An Analysis of

Ernst Kantorowicz's

The King's Two Bodies

T0301897

Simon Thomson

Published by Macat International Ltd
24:13 Coda Centre, 189 Munster Road, London SW6 6AW.

Distributed exclusively by Routledge
2 Park Square, Milton Park, Abingdon, Oxon OX14 4RN
711 Third Avenue, New York, NY 10017, USA

Routledge is an imprint of the Taylor & Francis Group, an informa business

www.macat.com
info@macat.com

Cataloguing in Publication Data
A catalogue record for this book is available from the British Library.
Library of Congress Cataloguing-in-Publication Data is available upon request.
Cover illustration: Etienne Gilfillan

ISBN 978-1-912302-67-3 (hardback)
ISBN 978-1-912127-11-5 (paperback)
ISBN 978-1-912281-55-8 (e-book)

Notice
The information in this book is designed to orientate readers of the work under analysis,
to elucidate and contextualise its key ideas and themes, and to aid in the development
of critical thinking skills. It is not meant to be used, nor should it be used, as a
substitute for original thinking or in place of original writing or research. References and
notes are provided for informational purposes and their presence does not constitute
endorsement of the information or opinions therein. This book is presented solely for
educational purposes. It is sold on the understanding that the publisher is not engaged
to provide any scholarly advice. The publisher has made every effort to ensure that
this book is accurate and up-to-date, but makes no warranties or representations with
regard to the completeness or reliability of the information it contains. The information
and the opinions provided herein are not guaranteed or warranted to produce particular
results and may not be suitable for students of every ability. The publisher shall not be
liable for any loss, damage or disruption arising from any errors or omissions, or from
the use of this book, including, but not limited to, special, incidental, consequential or
other damages caused, or alleged to have been caused, directly or indirectly, by the
information contained within.

CONTENTS

THE MACAT LIBRARY

The Macat Library is a series of unique academic explorations of seminal works in the humanities and social sciences – books and papers that have had a significant and widely recognised impact on their disciplines. It has been created to serve as much more than just a summary of what lies between the covers of a great book. It illuminates and explores the influences on, ideas of, and impact of that book. Our goal is to offer a learning resource that encourages critical thinking and fosters a better, deeper understanding of important ideas.

Each publication is divided into three Sections: Influences, Ideas, and Impact. Each Section has four Modules. These explore every important facet of the work, and the responses to it.

This Section-Module structure makes a Macat Library book easy to use, but it has another important feature. Because each Macat book is written to the same format, it is possible (and encouraged!) to cross-reference multiple Macat books along the same lines of inquiry or research. This allows the reader to open up interesting interdisciplinary pathways.

To further aid your reading, lists of glossary terms and people mentioned are included at the end of this book (these are indicated by an asterisk [*] throughout) – as well as a list of works cited.

Macat has worked with the University of Cambridge to identify the elements of critical thinking and understand the ways in which six different skills combine to enable effective thinking.
Three allow us to fully understand a problem; three more give us the tools to solve it. Together, these six skills make up the **PACIER** model of critical thinking. They are:

ANALYSIS – understanding how an argument is built
EVALUATION – exploring the strengths and weaknesses of an argument
INTERPRETATION – understanding issues of meaning

CREATIVE THINKING – coming up with new ideas and fresh connections
PROBLEM-SOLVING – producing strong solutions
REASONING – creating strong arguments

To find out more, visit **WWW.MACAT.COM.**

CRITICAL THINKING AND *THE KING'S TWO BODIES*

Primary critical thinking skill: EVALUATION
Secondary critical thinking skill: CREATIVE THINKING

Few historians trace grand themes across many centuries and places, but Ernst Kantorowicz's great work on the symbolic powers of kingship is a fine example of what can happen when they do.

The King's Two Bodies is at once a superb example of the critical thinking skill of evaluation – assessing huge quantities of evidence, both written and visual, and drawing sound comparative conclusions from it – and of creative thinking; the work connects art history, literature, legal records and historical documents together in innovative and revealing ways across more than 800 years of history.

Kantorowicz's key conclusions (that history is at root about ideas, that these ideas power institutions, and that both are commonly expressed and understood through symbols) have had a profound impact on several different disciplines, and even underpin many works of popular fiction – not least *The DaVinci Code*. And they were all made possible by fresh evaluation of evidence that other historians had ignored, or could not see the significance of.

ABOUT THE AUTHOR OF THE ORIGINAL WORK

Ernst Kantorowicz was born in 1895 in Posen. He served in the German army in World War I before opting for an academic career as a historian. That career was interrupted by the rise of the Nazi party in 1933. As a Jew, Kantorowicz was targeted, lost his job and decided to leave for England, moving on to the United States in 1939. There he experienced further persecution when, in 1949, he was fired from the University of Berkeley after refusing on principle to take an oath of loyalty to the US. Nevertheless, Kantorowicz eventually went on to work at both Harvard and Princeton. He died in 1963, aged 68.

ABOUT THE AUTHOR OF THE ANALYSIS

Dr Simon Thomson teaches at the Ruhr-Universität Bochum. He received his doctorate in medieval literature from University College London and is the editor, with M.D.J. Brintley, of *Sensory Perception in the Medieval World: Manuscripts, Texts and Other Material Matters.*

ABOUT MACAT

GREAT WORKS FOR CRITICAL THINKING

Macat is focused on making the ideas of the world's great thinkers accessible and comprehensible to everybody, everywhere, in ways that promote the development of enhanced critical thinking skills.

It works with leading academics from the world's top universities to produce new analyses that focus on the ideas and the impact of the most influential works ever written across a wide variety of academic disciplines. Each of the works that sit at the heart of its growing library is an enduring example of great thinking. But by setting them in context – and looking at the influences that shaped their authors, as well as the responses they provoked – Macat encourages readers to look at these classics and game-changers with fresh eyes. Readers learn to think, engage and challenge their ideas, rather than simply accepting them.

'Macat offers an amazing first-of-its-kind tool for interdisciplinary learning and research. Its focus on works that transformed their disciplines and its rigorous approach, drawing on the world's leading experts and educational institutions, opens up a world-class education to anyone.'

Andreas Schleicher
Director for Education and Skills, Organisation for Economic
Co-operation and Development

'Macat is taking on some of the major challenges in university education … They have drawn together a strong team of active academics who are producing teaching materials that are novel in the breadth of their approach.'

Prof Lord Broers,
former Vice-Chancellor of the University of Cambridge

'The Macat vision is exceptionally exciting. It focuses upon new modes of learning which analyse and explain seminal texts which have profoundly influenced world thinking and so social and economic development. It promotes the kind of critical thinking which is essential for any society and economy.
This is the learning of the future.'

Rt Hon Charles Clarke, former UK Secretary of State for Education

'The Macat analyses provide immediate access to the critical conversation surrounding the books that have shaped their respective discipline, which will make them an invaluable resource to all of those, students and teachers, working in the field.'

Professor William Tronzo, University of California at San Diego

WAYS IN TO THE TEXT

KEY POINTS

- Ernst Kantorowicz lived from 1895 to 1963. He was a German historian who specialized in medieval European politics.

- In *The King's Two Bodies*, he argues that medieval political and legal thinking used analogies relating to God and religious belief to understand and establish the power of the monarchy and other institutions. He also argues that the same thinking persists today and can still be seen in the construction of modern nationhood.

- The book has had a major impact on how works of literature and art are analyzed, particularly in terms of their social and political contexts. It is also an extraordinary collection of source material on medieval law.

Who Was Ernst Kantorowicz?

Born in 1895 in Posen (then in Germany, now in modern day Poland), Ernst Kantorowicz came from a wealthy family and took an interest in philosophy and politics from a young age. He published his first book in 1927 and seemed set for a glittering academic career.[1] When the Nazi* party took power in Germany in 1933, their strict rules about ethnic identities and political interests resulted in many academics being sacked. Because he was a Jew, Kantorowicz lost his job and left

Germany for England in 1938. In 1939 he moved to the United States to join the University of California at Berkeley. It was there that he started the work that would become *The King's Two Bodies: A Study in Medieval Political Theology*.

Even here, however, he faced political difficulties; in 1949 the Red Scare* (a fear of left-wing political thinkers) began in the US, and staff were required to take an oath of loyalty. Kantorowicz believed that the state should not interfere with academia, refused to sign, and was fired. By this stage, though, he was well known and went on to teach at Harvard University before becoming a member of the Institute for Advanced Study at Princeton in 1951. He stayed there, teaching and completing *The King's Two Bodies*, until illness forced his retirement in 1960. He died in 1963 aged 68 after an aneurism—an expansion and bursting of blood vessels that is particularly dangerous in the brain.

Without *The King's Two Bodies*, Kantorowicz would be remembered as one of a number of learned mid-twentieth-century legal and constitutional* historians, but this book makes him a key figure. It inspired a range of disciplines and became a constant feature in historical, artistic, and literary discussions.

What Does *The King's Two Bodies* Say?

Published in 1957, *The King's Two Bodies* is Ernst Kantorowicz's study of the medieval idea that a king has two bodies at the same time: a monarch is simultaneously a human being (that is, a physical person) and the representative of a country (that is, an abstract idea).

Kantorowicz refuses to mock the idea as earlier historians had done. Instead, he asks what a two-bodied king* meant "in its proper setting of medieval thought and political theory,"[2] and why it was so significant in that context. Kantorowicz shows that it is just one example of the use of religious ideas for political ends. He calls this political theology.*

Few academics write about political theology* today. But the book remains important, and is currently in its seventh reprint. There are French, Spanish, Portuguese, German, Italian, and Polish translations. In 2014, 57 years after publication, 93 articles referred to Kantorowicz's book. So why is that?

The book's most important idea is about the construction of power. It shows that symbols, literature, and art can make power. It also explores how the same symbols work in different contexts. This field, called semantics,* underpins many academic fields today. Some of its most influential thinkers, such as Michel Foucault,* followed Kantorowicz. Their interest in human physicality comes, to some extent, from this text. Foucault explored how people work within systems that bring order to large groups by using language and the legal system. I n doing so he consistently focuses on human "needs and desires." That is, he considers life as a physical, embodied experience and is interested in how those systems control and manipulate people's physical bodies rather then their minds or their abstract ideas.[3]

Kantorowicz argues that nations, organizations, and the law itself are all fictional notions. This does not make them irrelevant or silly. It just means that people construct them with the same symbols as those in art and literature. He points out that, in the modern world, this matters in our understanding of how to control companies. We do not understand whether companies have ethical responsibilities, in the same way as people do. Similarly, we are not always sure what it means to belong to a nation or what a country's identity is. *The King's Two Bodies* shows us how language and art can shape the meaning of an organization, a country, and of power.

Why Does *The King's Two Bodies* Matter?

The King's Two Bodies appears to have an extremely specific use. Its subtitle, "A Study in Medieval Political Theology," does not appeal to a wide audience. Political theology is a narrow field, even among medieval historians. Yet the book has influenced a wide range of readers. It describes a tension between physical existence and legal status. This, and the compelling central image of the "curious legal fiction of The King's Two Bodies,"[4] has interested students of art and literature, but much in this book has wider applications.

Kantorowicz does not see nations as real, but as invented ideas. Nor does he see history as a progressive development of civilization. Instead, he regards it as a continuous story of the making and employment of power. Kantorowicz reads any work of art as a political act. This means there is no fundamental truth. There is only the making of different meanings as they are useful in new contexts.

The King's Two Bodies, then, focuses on the ways that law, literature, and art can construct meaning—the process of semantics. The book identifies the same symbols in different times and places, and explores how their meanings can either vary or stay the same. Kantorowicz shows how ideas that appear limited can move into new contexts and form part of wider arguments.

The role of an abbot in a monastery, for example, can provide justification for the execution of a king.

In seventeenth-century England, opponents of the king, Charles I, had a problem. Although they wanted to execute him, both secular (worldly) and theological (religious) law said that Charles was king by the will of God. To have him killed, or even to fight against him, would be a crime against both God and the country.

But the same problem had been faced long before by the medieval Church. While an abbot is the head of a holy household and represents God's authority, sometimes abbots behaved badly and needed to be removed. A monk's disobedience could be justified if that monk could show that by disobeying the individual human abbot he was, in fact, obeying the authority *represented* by the abbot. So Charles's enemies used the idea of the king's two bodies to justify their actions. They showed they were not acting against the monarchy, or God, or the country. They were acting against the actual physical person of Charles Stuart.

The King's Two Bodies invites readers to follow its approach by taking ideas and applying them in new fields. This makes it a truly universal work.

NOTES

1   Ernst Kantorowicz, *Frederick the Second 1194–1250,* trans. E. O. Lorimer (New York: Frederick Ungar, 1957).

2   Ernst Kantorowicz, *The King's Two Bodies: A Study in Medieval Political Theology* (Princeton, NJ: Princeton University Press, 1997), 6.

3   Michel Foucault, *Order of Things: Archaeology of the Human Sciences* (London: Routledge,1989), 244.

SECTION 1
INFLUENCES

MODULE 1
THE AUTHOR AND THE HISTORICAL CONTEXT

KEY POINTS

- *The King's Two Bodies* significantly influenced twentieth-century analyses of literature and art. It explores how abstract ideas and symbols can be used to construct power at a national level.

- The appalling abuses of national power that took place during and after World War II* shaped Kantorowicz's concerns about how power is established and how history is understood.

- Ernst Kantorowicz had negative experiences of state power in Adolf Hitler's* Germany and in the United States during the Cold War.* These experiences helped form his analysis of how political power was created in the medieval period.

Why Read This Text?

In his 1957 book *The King's Two Bodies*, Ernst Kantorowicz examines the language and imagery used by medieval* lawyers exploring or justifying the power of their rulers.

From this basic description the text might appear to be of very limited interest. However, Kantorowicz's main image of a medieval ruler with "two bodies" (simultaneously a physical person and the abstract idea of a nation) has contributed to making the work very influential in a range of fields.

In the course of discussing what it means for a king to have two bodies, and the circumstances in which this concept was used across eight centuries of Western European* history, Kantorowicz explores

❝ Only hesitatingly and rarely did the author find it necessary to draw conclusions or indicate how the various topics in these pages should be geared with each other; but the reader will find it easy enough for himself to draw his own conclusions and himself combine the cogwheels, an operation facilitated by very numerous cross-references and a full index. **❞**

Ernst Kantorowicz, describing his own approach to *The King's Two Bodies: A Study in Medieval Political Theology*

much wider questions. His examination of legal procedure becomes far broader as he explores how nations, power, and meaning are all created. The conclusion he comes to— and the methodology that shapes his text—is that all these things are constructed by language and symbols, and that examples of the same words and images can be found in very different contexts. As a result, his text is as much about semantics*—the study of meaning and how meaning comes about— as it is about medieval kingship.

Kantorowicz's argument is backed up by plenty of evidence and examples, many of which focus on the king's body both in terms of the physical and in terms of its role as the representative of the nation.

The King's Two Bodies can be read as a mine of interesting cultural facts; as a study of kingship and medieval history; as a grand survey sweeping through time and space; and (most commonly today) as a study of how power is shaped by culture and language.

Author's Life

The King's Two Bodies was published in 1957. Although Kantorowicz was then working in Princeton University in the United States, he was Polish by birth and had spent his formative years in Germany. In his youth, Kantorowicz became involved in some far-right political groups and his political sympathies remained broadly right wing.

His move into medieval history seems to have been a result of the influence of his German lecturers Karl Hampe* and Friedrich Baethgen.* The poet Stefan George* probably influenced him, too, by exploring the use of mystical (spiritual) and religious language in matters of power and statehood.

Kantorowicz's first book, published in 1927, was about the German king Frederick II,* and can be seen as a celebration of German nationalism entirely in keeping with George's poetry.[1] Its publication was followed by a move to the University of Frankfurt, where he seemed set for a successful academic career.

This was interrupted, however, by the rise of the Nazi* party in Germany. Kantorowicz was Jewish and the racial policies of the Nazis (many of which focused on hatred of Jews) meant he was forced out of work in 1933. After spending a few years in a state of limbo, he left Germany for good in 1938. Like many of his colleagues, Kantorowicz went briefly to England, where he worked at the University of Oxford, before moving to the United States and the University of California at Berkeley in 1939. It was there that he developed the thinking that would become the basis of *The King's Two Bodies*.

Once again, government interference saw Kantorowicz leave a university institution. In 1949, he and 30 colleagues refused to take an oath of loyalty to the United States as a protest against what Kantorowicz saw as unjustified state interference in the world of academia. He was promptly fired. By this stage, though, being already fairly well known, he managed to find work in other institutions. Kantorowicz briefly taught at Harvard University before joining the Institute for Advanced Study at Princeton University in 1951. Here he stayed, working on medieval and early modern constitutional* and legal history until illness forced his retirement in 1960. Ernst Kantorowicz died in 1963 at the age of 68.

Author's Background

When the Nazi party took power in Germany in 1933, their racial and political ideology resulted in the dismissal of a large number of academics from their academic posts, because either their political views or their ethnic identities were considered unacceptable. Kantorowicz's family was Jewish, and so he was forced out of his job. By the time the Nazis' extermination of Jewish people and other groups—including homosexuals, black people, and gypsies—was understood to be a deliberate policy, Kantorowicz was already living in the United States.[2]

But 16 years after being forced out of the University of Frankfurt, Kantorowicz experienced a different form of government persecution. In 1949, the ideological standoff between the United States and the Soviet Union* (what became known as the Cold War) had just started. The United States was terrified of communism* and the "Red Scare"* began. This was a period of great paranoia where many felt the country had to root out anti-American feeling and behavior in its society in order to stop communists gaining a foothold. The movement became known as McCarthyism,* because one of its most vocal supporters was the American Senator Joseph McCarthy.* The academic community in California was under pressure to show patriotism and Kantorowicz and his colleagues at the University of California were asked to take an oath of loyalty. Many refused, including Kantorowicz, and for this he was dismissed.

Since the Enlightenment* period of the seventeenth and eighteenth centuries, European academia assumed that human society was defined by progression.[3] This meant that history should be understood as a continuous development and improvement in the way people understand and organize both themselves and the world as they become ever more civilized.

Progress, then, could be measured using a scientific approach based on observation and logical conclusions—and once the idea had taken root that history was not simply a sequence of events but a progression, that idea was then applied to all aspects of society.

This, however, was not Kantorowicz's experience of life at all, as his experiences in both Germany and the United States showed. And it was not how he saw either history or art in *The King's Two Bodies*. As Kantorowicz drily noted, "Horrors justified by the names of God or *patria* are as old as they are new."[4] This understanding led him to argue against an "optimistic philosophy of unlimited progress."[5]

NOTES

1   For a useful discussion of the politics of this work, see Martin Ruehl, "In This Time Without Emperors: The Politics of Ernst Kantorowicz's *Friedrich der Zweite* Reconsidered," *Journal of the Warburg and Courtauld Institutes* 63 (2000): 187–242.

2   For a discussion of the Holocaust and some of Kantorowicz's ideas, see Uriel Tal, "On Structures of Political Theology and Myth Prior to the Holocaust," in *The Holocaust as Historical Experience,* ed. Yehuda Bauer and Nathan Rotenstreich (New York: Holmes and Meier, 1981), 43–74.

3   For a contemporary discussion of the Enlightenment in sympathy with Kantorowicz's approach, see Ernst Cassirer, *The Philosophy of the Enlightenment*, trans. Fritz C. A. Koelln and James P. Pettegrove (Princeton, NJ: Princeton University Press, 1964).

4   Ernst Kantorowicz, *The King's Two Bodies: A Study in Medieval Political Theology* (Princeton, NJ: Princeton University Press, 1997), 246.

5   Kantorowicz, *The King's Two Bodies*, 274.

MODULE 2
ACADEMIC CONTEXT

KEY POINTS

- The King's Two Bodies brings together what academics working in this area of history were thinking about in the first and second halves of the twentieth century.

- Kantorowicz wanted to broaden historical study. He rejected the idea of history as a progressive series of events and argued that historians should study sociological and cultural ideas and change.

- Kantorowicz was influenced by the work of the political theologist* Carl Schmitt* and applied his ideas to the discipline.

The Work in Its Context

Although the core ideas of Ernst Kantorowicz's *The King's Two Bodies: A Study in Medieval Political Theology* are firmly rooted in the ideas of early twentieth-century historians, it is a comprehensive work that pays close attention to primary sources across a long period of time.

While the work generally follows in the tradition of nineteenth-century historians such as F.W. Maitland,* its examination of political structures and how they come about reflects both the thinking of Kantorowicz's contemporaries such as the political theorist Carl Schmitt* and his own understanding of statehood and power. Kantorowicz looks closely at the notion of political theology* (that is, the ways in which states and rulers use mythical and religious language and structures to exert power over their subjects). He was interested in this concept having witnessed the growth of authoritarian regimes in twentieth-century Europe.

❝ Modern self-conscious reflection on the political use of sociology ... brought with it an approving revival of the term 'political theology' ... [and] signified a reactionary theology of history taking into account the most modern sociology—a mixture of viewpoints that eventually was to open perspectives on the possibilities of cynical self-deception as a way of synthesizing mythical antidotes to decadent unbelief. ❞

John Stroup, from his 1987 essay "Political Theology and Secularization Theory in Germany, 1918–1939: Emmanuel Hirsch as a Phenomenon of His Time"

But *The King's Two Bodies* is also a work that was ahead of its time. It looked at the link between cultural phenomena and the work of actual people, anticipating approaches that would come to dominate academic thought in the 1960s and 1970s by writers such as the French sociologist Michel Foucault.*

By seeing the production of literature and art as political acts, *The King's Two Bodies* laid the foundations for the work of New Historicists* such as Stephen Greenblatt.* New Historicism is a literary movement, important in the 1980s and 1990s, that considers how and why texts were produced when they were and the shifts in their meanings over time given changing historical contexts. To a degree, then, *The King's Two Bodies* is a bridge between the main areas of academic interest of the first and second halves of the twentieth century.

Overview of the Field

Kantorowicz wanted to make the study of history wider and more complex, something more than simply the process of identifying what events happened when. In this he was following the work of French historian Marc Bloch.* In his studies of French rural history, Bloch rejected the idea of a simple event-based history and argued that the study of sociological and cultural ideas and change would yield much better results. The notion in *The King's Two Bodies* that ideas have a life of their own builds on Bloch's work.

The King's Two Bodies was not the first piece of writing to focus on the idea of a king having two bodies, of him being both a physical person and a symbol of the state. In his introduction to the book, Kantorowicz summarizes the dismissive views of other historians, including Maitland, towards this idea. While he admits to the "seemingly ludicrous, and in many respects awkward, concept of the King's Two Bodies,"[1] Kantorowicz's intention is not to look at the concept through modern eyes. He is looking to fathom it on its own terms and so enable modern readers to understand both the challenge and the opportunity it presented to medieval* thinkers.

Academic Influences

Kantorowicz was not the first writer to think of the idea of political theology* (a concept that looks at how systems of power can be based on the same ideas as religion). In most cultures, religious ideas come before social, economic, and governance structures, historically speaking. This means that the language and symbolism used by religion are both relatively sophisticated and powerful. Most early medieval rulers based their authority on the threat of what they could do with their power and on how wealth was distributed. Naturally, however, this restricted the areas and the numbers of people they could control. The movement from this localized exercise of power to the more ambitious construction of nations is complex. Moreover, rulers found they could extend their control and influence over larger areas and more people by using the same intellectual ideas of religion and the language that accompanied it. Political theology analyzes this idea.[2]

The concept of political theology* was keenly discussed during Kantorowicz's early academic career in Germany. He was very aware of conversations people were having about the country's government—known as the Weimar Republic*—and the rise of Adolf Hitler's Nazi* party through the 1930s. The historians Percy Ernst Schramm* and Carl Erdmann* were working in this area at this time. Kantorowicz borrowed the phrase "political theology" from Carl Schmitt's 1922 book of the same name;[3] Schmitt's analysis that "all significant concepts of the modern theory of the state are secularized theological concepts" can be seen as the foundation of the ideas contained in *The King's Two Bodies*.[4] Kantorowicz's thinking is closely linked to Schmitt's ideas about how states make power, although his study is more historical than philosophical.

The German philosopher Ernst Cassirer* also had a significant influence on *The King's Two Bodies*. Cassirer's final work, *The Myth of the State*, was published in 1946.[5] In it he explored how states use cultural forms to construct myths about themselves, and his work was very influential as people started a philosophical discussion about Nazism. Kantorowicz seems to have used Cassier's book to start a wider debate about how this kind of myth-making works.

NOTES

1   Ernst Kantorowicz, *The King's Two Bodies* (Princeton, NJ: Princeton University Press 1997), 5.

2   For a modern discussion of political theology, see Hent de Vries and Lawrence E. Sullivan, eds, *Political Theologies* (New York: Fordham University Press, 2006).

3   Carl Schmitt, *Political Theology: Four Chapters on the History of Sovereignty*, trans. George Schwab (Cambridge, MA: MIT Press, 1985), 36.

4   See Victoria Kahn, "Political Theology and Fiction in *The King's Two Bodies*," *Representations* 106, no. 1 (2009): 79. Here Kahn quotes this famous statement in the same context of exploring Kantorowicz's learning from and response to Schmitt.

5   Ernst Cassirer, *The Myth of the State* (New Haven, CT: Yale University Press, 1946).

MODULE 3
THE PROBLEM

KEY POINTS

- Kantorowicz explores how images and symbols are used to construct ideas of nationhood, and how they can control people.

- Most historians saw the writing of history as the recording of events and the actions of significant individuals.

- Kantorowicz wanted to write a history of ideas rather than events, to show that the same ideas recur throughout history, and to show that power has always been exerted through the use of symbols.

Core Question

The core question that Ernst Kantorowicz begins with in *The King's Two Bodies* is how the medieval* period understood kingship and nationhood. He finds that it focused on the use of images and symbols, particularly the key image of a king simultaneously having two bodies—one physical and one abstract. So Kantorowicz's core question shifts to asking where that particular image came from and how it was represented in different contexts and different times.

This was not an original question. How nations shaped themselves and the role of kingship in that process had been discussed before. Kantorowicz himself had looked at some of the issues 30 years before *The King's Two Bodies*, when he wrote about the medieval German king Frederick II* and his role in shaping his country. In some senses, the question at the center of Kantorowicz's book had already been answered by the time he wrote it. He seems to have seen it as a guide rather than a groundbreaking revelation of a new idea. Previous and

> ❝ This study may be taken among other things as an attempt to understand and, if possible, demonstrate how, by what means and methods, certain axioms of a political theology which *mutatis mutandis* [with the necessary changes having been made] was to remain valid until the twentieth century, began to be developed during the later Middle Ages. ❞
>
> Ernst Kantorowicz, *The King's Two Bodies: A Study in Medieval Political Theology*

contemporary historians had already explored the role of law in shaping rulers and nations. They had considered the importance of religious imagery in politics and they had identified the idea of a modern state as rooted in medieval myth.

So Kantorowicz's book was not really answering a question at all. It was providing the final, comprehensive, contribution to a debate.

The book did address a more controversial issue, though—that of historiography (that is, exactly how history should be written). In this area *The King's Two Bodies* offers an unusual mixture. On the one hand, it is a grand survey of time and place. On the other, it also examines a concept in detail, taking all types of evidence into account, including the particular circumstances of the individuals he focuses on. To a certain degree Kantorowicz offers a new way of writing history. He uses an academic methodology that deals with the past, the present, and the future and with *presentation* more the focus than *events*.

The Participants

Kantorowicz had been taught by the German historians Friedrich Baethgen* and Karl Hampe.* Like Kantorowicz, Baethgen was interested in how the literary arts and religion might be used to better understand historical issues of rulership. Hampe, meanwhile, worked on the development of the modern German state in the thirteenth century. *The King's Two Bodies* investigates both approaches to the medieval. It takes on the religious and literary interests of Baethgen, as well as Hampe's focus on the building of a state.

The political theorist Carl Schmitt,* who was writing before Kantorowicz and worked with the Nazi* regime in the 1950s, coined the phrase "political theology"[1] and Kantorowicz is clearly interested in this area too.[2] Prominent Nazis, including Adolf Hitler* and Joseph Goebbels,* were keen on Schmitt's principles of political theology. After the defeat of Nazism in World War II,* any idea that was closely tied to the Nazis was viewed as highly suspect. As a result, political theology has become tainted both as a phrase and an idea; this has, in turn, affected Kantorowicz's reputation. He has even been described by the medieval historian Norman Cantor* as a "Nazi twin" in an influential analysis of his work.[3]

Kantorowicz works with his period and subject matter in a similar way to the early twentieth-century American historian Charles Beard.* Beard controversially argued that individual economic interests dominated how the American constitution was put together. Kantorowicz, too, focuses on individuals and their immediate goals, as well as on economics and its influence on the history of ideas. But he also follows earlier historians such as F. W. Maitland* by writing to cover a vast sweep of time. The German sociologist Reinhard Bendix* found a similar methodological approach to Kantorowicz by putting different contexts next to one another in comparative historical studies.

The Contemporary Debate

Kantorowicz sets out the important areas of his thinking at the very start of the text. He reveals that he first considered the idea of the king's two bodies* in a conversation with his colleague, the legal scholar Max Radin,* when they worked together in California.

They were talking about the relationship between religion and law in contemporary America and then turned to the idea of "the abstract 'crown' as a corporation"[4]—that is, the idea of similarities between the legal statuses of royalty and corporations. F. W. Maitland had written about this in 1901, particularly in relation to the early modern* idea of the king's two bodies. The early modern period is generally understood to run from around 1500 to around 1800.

Kantorowicz acknowledges the importance of Maitland's work. His other major source is Carl Schmitt's* 1922 book on political theology.[5] In it, Schmitt set the terms for Kantorowicz's discussion of how imagery is used by the state, arguing in favor of the value and validity of the cultural promotion of nationalism. Writing later, Kantorowicz felt less need to defend how states shape themselves, but he was still interested in the same questions.

Yet perhaps the most useful text to read to give *The King's Two Bodies* some context is Kantorowicz's own earlier work *Frederick The Second, 1194–1250*. In it he considers questions about how power was wielded with the use of religious language and symbols. And Kantorowicz continued to think about what makes a state on every level—legal, religious, historical, artistic, and literary.

It is perhaps best to look at *The King's Two Bodies* as an accumulation of learning rather than as a work that you can use to actively participate in a contemporary debate.

NOTES

1   See also Uriel Tal, "On Structures of Political Theology and Myth Prior to the Holocaust," in *The Holocaust as Historical Experience,* ed. Yehuda Bauer and Nathan Rotenstreich (New York: Holmes and Meier, 1981), 43–74.

2   For discussions of Schmitt and Nazism, see Norman Cantor, "The Nazi Twins: Percy Ernst Schramm and Ernst Hartwig Kantorowicz," in *Inventing the Middle Ages: The Lives, Works, and Ideas of the Great Medievalists of the Twentieth Century,* ed. Norman Cantor (New York: Harper Collins, 1991), 79–117, and David Bates, "Theology and the Nazi State: Carl Schmitt's Concept of the Institution," *Modern Intellectual History* 3 (2006): 415–42.

3   Cantor, "The Nazi Twins."

4   Ernst Kantorowicz, *The King's Two Bodies* (Princeton, NJ: Princeton University Press, 1997), xxi.

5   Carl Schmitt, *Political Theology: Four Chapters on the Concept of Sovereignty,* trans. George D. Schwab (Cambridge, MA: MIT Press, 1985). Originally published as Carl Schmitt, *Politische Theologie. Vier Kapitel zur Lehre von der Souveränität* (Berlin: Duncker & Humblot, 1922).

MODULE 4
THE AUTHOR'S CONTRIBUTION

KEY POINTS

- The notion of the king's two bodies* is an example of a legal understanding based on theology.* The idea was used to help medieval* nation states function.

- Partly as a result of *The King's Two Bodies*, historians have become much more focused on ideas and on how events took place rather than simply recording what happened.

- Kantorowicz was deeply influenced by contemporaries such as Carl Schmitt* and Ernst Cassirer,* who were also interested in politics and statehood.

Author's Aims

Although *The King's Two Bodies* does not present a new historical concept, the work is original in the scope and breadth of Ernst Kantorowicz's thinking.

His ideas about how power is built up in states are rooted in the thinking of contemporaries such as Carl Schmitt and Ernst Cassirer, and his historiographical scale—that is, his interest in writing about history across a huge sweep of time—has similarities to the approach of the legal historian F. W. Maitland.* Indeed, Kantorowicz does not claim to be creating anything original,d nor does he say he is producing a definitive argument. Instead, he seems to view the book as a storehouse for the knowledge he has accumulated throughout his career.[1] He thinks of it as a teaching text, designed "in view of the needs of students,"[2] rather than as a groundbreaking work of original scholarship.

However, his confidence in handling these sources means he is able to do something innovative. He moves away from a chronological

> ❝ The seemingly irrational maxims ... were partly the
> result of the adaptation of theological language and
> thought to the new conditions of the secular state, and
> partly the result of the establishment of an impersonal
> public sphere which emerged from the proper needs of
> the community of the realm itself. ❞
>
> Ernst Kantorowicz, *The King's Two Bodies: A Study in Medieval Political Theology*

account of events—that is, describing the events in the order they
occurred—and explores instead the thought of the period he is
looking at. His focus on the king's physical body and then the
differences he goes on to draw between different types of bodies—
and their respective values—are not unique but the scale on which he
delivers it is. He also brings ideas of physicality to the center of
academic discussion.[3] Kantorowicz covers literature, the visual arts,
and public performance with equal confidence. This makes the book
relevant to academics in different fields, opening up unexpected
connections between disciplines.

As a result, *The King's Two Bodies* starts to be much more about
how language and symbols contribute to the forming of ideas and
meaning, and much less about what happened and how it happened.
This was a challenging approach. Critics recognized the value of the
sources, but did not always find it easy to identify exactly what the
book as a whole was *about*. Some people found it "a rich and muddled"
work which "confuses because the author ... follows neither a
chronological nor a systematic order."[4]

Approach

Kantorowicz describes his study as "an attempt to understand and, if
possible, demonstrate how, by what means and methods, certain
axioms of a political theology ... began to be developed during the

later Middle Ages."[5] He often states that he sees *The King's Two Bodies* as an exploration of just one aspect of the wide and complex issue of power and how it is held. He intends "to outline the historical problem" of the dual body of the monarch and help future students to consider it further.[6]

He often cites and discusses classical thinkers (that is, thinkers of the Greek and Roman period), particularly lawyers, while the historical period he looks at runs from the ninth-century court of Charlemagne* in northern Germany to the mid-seventeenth-century trial of Charles I* in London. The image of the king's two bodies becomes Kantorowicz's tool to control his material. He returns to it many times, building most of his chapters and sections around the idea.

The King's Two Bodies starts by examining the dual nature—physical and conceptual—of the body that lawyers had claimed for the English king Edward VI,* crowned king when he was just nine years old. Later chapters explore different ways of representing kings, each time exploring this idea of duality.* Kantorowicz also identifies how a theoretical concept in law or in religion was represented in literature or art at the same time. His major redefinition of the question of kingship was to argue that the same image systems work across different media— philosophy, theology, administrative law, constitutional law, drama, poetry, and the visual arts. This is what he terms "constitutional semantics."*

Contribution in Context

Kantorowicz belonged to a set of educated mid-twentieth-century constitutional historians* that included his teachers Friedrich Baethgen* and Karl Hampe* and the historian F. W. Maitland, whose work on the idea of the king's two bodies* is considered in the introduction to Kantorowicz's book.[7] All of these people were working on questions about how the medieval* state had come to be established and the relationship between medieval and modern systems of

government. Kantorowicz's particular interest in political theology*
came from his German contemporaries Carl Schmitt and Ernst Cassirer.
Both belonged to a school of thought interested in the question of how
culture informs and shapes the power of the state.

Like Schmitt and Cassirer, Kantorowicz's thinking about how image
systems and religious ideas influence the development of laws and state
power came from his experiences in Germany in the 1920s and 1930s.
Kantorowicz was particularly influenced by the circle around the poet
Stefan George.* This circle included the literary scholar Friedrich
Gundolf,* whose ideas about the political significance of literature in
this area can be seen in *The King's Two Bodies*.

Kantorowicz's thinking was to a degree adapted from Schmitt and
Cassirer's conceptual ideas and then merged with the kind of historical
inquiry endorsed by F. W. Maitland. The text is original and
groundbreaking thanks to Kantorowicz's breadth of coverage and his
creative handling of a range of sources.

NOTES

1   See the comments made by Professor Michael Maloney in personal
correspondence to William Chester Jordan, preface to Ernst Kantorowicz,
The King's Two Bodies (Princeton, NJ: Princeton University Press, 1997), xiv;
compare Kantorowicz's own remarks in his own preface (Kantorowicz, *The
King's Two Bodies,* xviii).

2   Kantorowicz, *The King's Two Bodies*, xx.

3   See Michel Foucault, *Discipline and Punish: The Birth of the Prison,* 2nd edn,
trans. Alan Sheridan (New York: Vintage, 1975), in which Foucault* claims to
be working "in homage to Kantorowicz."

4   Beryl Smalley, review of *The King's Two Bodies* by Ernst Kantorowicz, *Past &
Present* 20 (1961): 30.

5   Kantorowicz, *The King's Two Bodies*, xviii.

6   Kantorowicz, *The King's Two Bodies*, 6.

7   Kantorowicz, *The King's Two Bodies*, 6.

SECTION 2
IDEAS

MODULE 5
MAIN IDEAS

KEY POINTS

- Kantorowicz is interested in how power was understood and developed in medieval* Europe, and particularly in the language and symbols used in its pursuit.

- The text argues that power is constructed by the artful use of symbols, which are often connected with bodies and physicality.

- *The King's Two Bodies* finds similar concerns and expressions across a long period of history and in different disciplines and media.

Key Themes

Ernst Kantorowicz's *The King's Two Bodies* explores how the power of kings was understood in medieval Europe. His most influential idea lies in how he approaches this concept: it is his methodology,* rather than his conclusions, that make the work important.

In exploring how laws make power, however, he repeatedly returns to three themes: the use of primarily religious symbols and ideas in making power; the relationship between art, literature, and law and physicality; and the way meaning shifts in different contexts.

Kantorowicz shows that the power of medieval rulers was often defined by thinking developed in the Church. He finds lawyers and artists working on behalf of rulers who come up with useful religious ideas to justify extensions of power, such as for the king's control of the land. This use of religious ideas for political needs is called "political theology."*[1]

Kantorowicz's main example of how political theology is used is that of the king's two bodies.* Originally used to explain Christ's

66 One constructed a corporate person, a kind of *persona mystica,* which was a collective only and exclusively with regard to Time, since the plurality of its members was made up only and exclusively by succession ... That is, one constructed a body corporate ... a mystical person by perpetual devolution whose mortal and temporary incumbent was of relatively minor importance as compared to the immortal body corporate by succession which he represented. 99

Ernst Kantorowicz, *The King's Two Bodies: A Study in Medieval Political Theology*

existence as both man and God, the idea was then applied to rulers for political purposes. The idea is that a monarch is at one and the same time a *physical person* and an *abstract idea*: both a human being and a representation of a country. But this is not a metaphor.* The king's body does not *symbolize* the nation. Rather, the king *is* both flesh and country at the same time.

Kantorowicz's third theme, of how meaning shifts according to context, focuses on how the same image can be put to different uses. *The King's Two Bodies* ranges from the coronation of the Holy Roman Emperor Charlemagne* in Rome in 800 to the execution of the English king Charles I* in London in 1649. The book discusses philosophy, theology, administrative law, constitutional law, drama, poetry, and visual arts. This span of time and medium allows Kantorowicz to show that the same symbol can be made to mean different things at different times.

The idea of the king's two bodies was used both by monarchs and by those who opposed them in the following way. A monarch could claim to represent a mystical, "legally eternal" power embodying and representing the whole state. This "body" was divine. The second body, a body of flesh and blood, represented the divine body on earth; the divine body lent this "real" body the unopposable right to accrue authority and wealth. But a monarch's opponent could, by the same logic, claim that if a monarch had two bodies, it was possible to oppose the earthly, material monarch while supporting the divine monarch. Kantorowicz calls this reuse of the same image to illustrate different ideas about power "constitutional semantics."*

Exploring the Ideas

The King's Two Bodies is not a single argument leading to a conclusion. It is a series of explorations of one issue from different angles. Its cohesion lies in its analysis of the concept of kingship, and in its consistent investigation into semantics.* There are linking paragraphs at the start and end of chapters but these may seem artificial—an attempt to show that a series of essays around one idea can be seen as a coherent work.

In part, this is because *The King's Two Bodies* deliberately considers all of medieval Europe as a single entity. Kantorowicz assumes that a lawyer writing in Normandy in 1100 can have a conversation with writers working for Charlemagne* in 800 or politicians looking to remove their king in 1649. This is a diachronic analysis (that is, an analysis where a single issue is considered across different periods) rather than a synchronic analysis (that is, an analysis which examines exactly what was happening at a specific time).

In the same way, the book also sees different media as taking part in a single conversation. It assumes that lawyers and dramatists, sculptors and monks, painters, monarchs, and poets all share similar concerns, and so draws on a huge range of sources, from sculpture on the tombs of French kings to Shakespeare's* plays. This approach has resulted in the book's most significant impact on later scholarship: an interest in semantic analysis, how signs and symbols can create meaning. Kantorowicz is interested in how similar symbols (words or visual images) are used by different people and how those symbols and their meanings vary from context to context, from place to place, and from medium to medium.

Language and Expression

Kantorowicz wrote of himself, "Only hesitatingly and rarely did the author find it necessary to draw conclusions or indicate how the various topics in these pages should be ... [integrated] with each other."[2] This is true, *The King's Two Bodies* is a mine of evidence rather than a continuous argument. To counterbalance this, Kantorowicz presents his work as a progressive analysis, making exclamations such as "at last" and "we now understand."[3]

Regardless of Kantorowicz's intention, readers can safely choose those chapters that interest them, or select those that fit with other programs of study, and follow the threads that appeal. Historically, this is how the book has mainly been read and that is why different chapters have influenced different fields.

This is not, however, the only aspect in which the book is challenging. Kantorowicz wanted to create a reference book for future study.[4] As a result, the quantity of primary information in *The King's Two Bodies* means the author's references sometimes overwhelm his discussion. In *The King's Two Bodies* you find the language of law, literature, art, religion, and political history. It presents 800 years of history as a unified period. And it shows how language and symbols are used to create meaning and power, rather than analyzing that power in action. This is always impressive—but it can be dizzying.

The author's asides to the reader do give the sense that he is guiding us, though, almost as if the reader were in a seminar. Flashes of humor and elegant expressions and the confident handling of primary material give a sense of security. Kantorowicz never explains how and why the work is structured, it may be that he did not fully think this through. His account of the writing of *The King's Two Bodies* is that it grew out of a conversation, and that is often its tone.

Kantorowicz generally translates significant terms into English. But he is interested in word choice and readers need to understand the terms he uses to grasp the subtleties of the text. One example is the distinction he makes between the lower case "king" and the capitalized "King." For Kantorowicz, King with a capital "K" carries an abstract sense. It is the concept of a king, rather than the individual human who is a King.

He also uses Latin, French, or German terms where they suit his argument. One example is the Latin *patria*. This can be translated as "country," "nation" or "state." He prefers its relative vagueness to the more specific English terms and values its suggestion of "patriotism."

NOTES

1   For a modern discussion of political theology, see Hent de Vries and Lawrence E. Sullivan, eds, *Political Theologies* (New York: Fordham University Press, 2006).

2   Ernst Kantorowicz, *The King's Two Bodies* (Princeton, NJ: Princeton University Press, 1997), xxi.

3   Kantorowicz, *The King's Two Bodies*, 199, 241.

4   Kantorowicz, *The King's Two Bodies*, xx.

MODULE 6
SECONDARY IDEAS

KEY POINTS

- Kantorowicz's secondary ideas concern time, the legal status of individuals and corporations, and the ways in which art, especially literature, functions.

- *The King's Two Bodies* also explores how nations began to think of themselves as permanent.

- The historical value of *The King's Two Bodies* as a text that marked the end of a certain type of historical investigation has largely been overlooked.

Other Ideas

The secondary ideas that interest Ernst Kantorowicz in *The King's Two Bodies* concern issues that he sees as significant in the medieval* period.

One particular area of interest is physicality—that is, the understanding that objects can have a physical and an abstract existence at the same time. In his central argument, Kantorowicz applies the idea of physicality to a king's body. He goes on to apply the idea to other objects, such as the crown, too. His quotations and illustrations give many examples of the different ways in which the physicality of certain objects and beings has been represented. It this concept that seems particularly to have influenced the French philosopher Michel Foucault.*

Kantorowicz also explores the political aspect of literature—a line of inquiry that has been more influential than perhaps even he might have expected. A single relatively short chapter analyzing some aspects of William Shakespeare's* play *Richard II** has generated endless

❝ The most significant feature of the personified collectives and corporate bodies was that they projected into past and future, that they preserved their identity despite changes and that therefore they were legally immortal. ❞

Ernst Kantorowicz, *The King's Two Bodies: A Study in Medieval Political Theology*

studies and books. *The King's Two Bodies* is most cited today in relation to English drama from the early modern* period rather than in relation to the power of the medieval state.[1]

Beyond these two areas now considered important to readings of the text, *The King's Two Bodies* also looks into the wider cultural impact of the developments it describes. Kantorowicz explores how in his view the state's use of religious ideas altered the ways in which time itself was understood in medieval Europe. He also considered the similarity in the ways in which post-medieval businesses and the medieval monarchy both functioned.

Exploring the Ideas

A key strand that runs throughout Kantorowicz's analysis is "a change of man's sense of the nature of Time."[2] Time is an issue that keeps coming up when he discusses the differences between an eternal God and temporary men, the differences between the brief life that God gives to His creation and the theoretical eternity of institutions created by man, and the differences between the notion of eternal kingship and the actual brief reigns and lives of humans.

Religious time, Kantorowicz explains, was as eternal as God. But for the early medieval state, time was appropriate to individual lives: that is, incidents were dealt with when they occurred, funds were raised through taxation for specific events, and possessions such as land were owned for an individual's lifetime.

If the king had both a mortal, physical body *and* a permanent mystical body, and if the permanent, divine body were indistinguishable from the state, then in some legal senses *both the king and the nation were permanent*.

A country was now a permanent thing. It existed in the past and in the future. Now taxation, for example, was an annually repeated demand; it would never end. As for time—time was permanent and continuous, too; it became a material with which humans could work, rather than the frame in which we are set.

Time takes center stage in the brief but remarkable sixth chapter, "On Continuity and Corporations." This section of *The King's Two Bodies* steps aside from forensic discussions of when and where different strands of the idea of dual-bodied rulers came from. Instead, it explores how nations themselves moved from being loose and temporary groups based on immediate circumstances into regarding themselves as permanent. Kantorowicz pragmatically ties this into the administration of national economics. He argues that "taxation, formerly linked to an unrepeatable event, now was linked to the calendar, to the eternally rolling wheel of Time. The state had become permanent."[3]

In the same section, Kantorowicz considers the status of businesses and corporations. He sees similarities between the legal innovations made to argue the case for a twin-bodied king and those which make "collectives and corporate bodies ... legally immortal."[4] Interestingly, he stresses the fictional nature of all of these models. So, as a state's needs and interests change, one "fiction ... yields to a new fiction."[5] This approach follows earlier writers such as Ernst Cassirer,* whose *Myth of the State* argues that any case a nation makes for its own identity and destiny is based on irrational and untrue stories. Unlike Cassirer, Kantorowicz is not opposed to states creating myths about themselves. He regards every attempt to construct a nation and its government as "fictional" in some sense.

Overlooked

Ironically for a book primarily concerned with history, *The King's Two Bodies* has perhaps had the least impact in the field of historical inquiry. It could be argued that its historical value has been overlooked. To some extent, this is because the academic world has been less focused on constitutional history in the 50 years since the book's publication than it was in the 50 years before it. So, in a way, the text's major concerns have been the most overlooked while its secondary themes have been explored in more detail.

The King's Two Bodies can be seen as marking the end of a certain type of historical investigation. To achieve its ends, it has to move rapidly across time and space, which does not allow detailed and contextualized analysis of each historical moment. It often feels as though Kantorowicz is *using* the people and events he mentions rather than actually contextualizing or analyzing them. The study of history since the book's publication has reacted against this style with increasingly narrow but extremely detailed studies that seek to provide the fullest possible contextualization and analysis.

A set of papers presented in 2007 both drew attention to the ways in which *The King's Two Bodies* has been used and suggested ways in which its relative neglect by historians might be put right.[6] Most of the papers continue to focus on Kantorowicz himself or on literary criticism, however, rather than on what he has to say about medieval or constitutional history. It is still too early to tell whether they have had any effect.

NOTES

1   At the time of writing, a search on the online academic resource JSTOR showed that ten of the 25 most recent studies citing *The King's Two Bodies* cited it in relation to literature and drama; only two cited it in relation to medieval history.

2   Ernst Kantorowicz, *The King's Two Bodies* (Princeton, NJ: Princeton University Press, 1997), 283.

3   Kantorowicz, *The King's Two Bodies*, 286.

4   Kantorowicz, *The King's Two Bodies*, 311.

5   Kantorowicz, *The King's Two Bodies*, 285.

6   The papers were presented at a panel held at the Renaissance Society of America's annual meeting in 2007. For an overview of both panel and papers, see Stephen Greenblatt, "Fifty Years of the *King's Two Bodies*," *Representations* 106, no. 1 (2009): 63–6.

ACHIEVEMENT

KEY POINTS

- Kantorowicz created a valuable sourcebook and a provocative exploration of how different media can be made to contribute towards political goals.

- *The King's Two Bodies* presents the accumulated notes of a career spent investigating primary sources, making it a rich and thoughtful work.

- Tremendously ambitious, the text is neither a comprehensive survey of medieval* political law nor a complete exploration of the use of symbols in the construction of state power. So while it is always interesting, it is often unconvincing in its detail.

Assessing the Argument

At the end of *The King's Two Bodies*, Ernst Kantorowicz offers an epilogue or an overall comment rather than a firm conclusion. Although we are still left with the complex idea of a king's two bodies,* we are much more richly informed about its history and purpose—and we have the tools both to identify and investigate other theological* ideas that have influenced political power.

It does not seem as though Kantorowicz wanted to reach any definitive conclusions about the nature of political theology.* It appears that he was more interested in producing a source for future investigations rather than a neat, definitive argument on the subject.

This shouldn't come as a surprise; Kantorowicz himself said that his work would be a sourcebook for students[1]—and so it proved for many years.[2] Today, of course, the Internet has transformed the way students access such sources. To some extent this makes his long

> ❝ [Constitutional semantics,] … the academic field he outlines in his book, has been systematically theorized only by the generation following him—by Reinhard Koselleck, Quentin Skinner, Jacques Guilhaumou, and others. Moreover, only today's scholars have the facilities needed to get from medieval texts the kind of information that Kantorowicz wished to obtain, and to perform the kind of studies in which Kantorowicz was interested. ❞
>
> Bernhard Jussen, "*The King's Two Bodies* Today"

quotations less relevant—particularly as they are often in Latin, and modern readers generally have less knowledge of the language than Kantorowicz's contemporaries. Nevertheless, his evidence has still spurred further research.

The author's skill in finding parallels and connections between widely differing sources has helped people develop their thinking about meaning and power in other nation states. But the broad range of the work can be confusing in scope. Over a few pages, the reader is taken from the German court of the ninth-century emperor Charlemagne* to the seventeenth-century trial of Charles I* in London and back again. For the modern reader looking to get to grips with medieval history this can be overwhelming.

In some ways, Kantorowicz achieved his main goal of interesting his readers in a certain period of history. It is unlikely however, that he would have expected the book to be used more by philosophers and literature students than by historians and it is equally unlikely that he would have foreseen the book becoming far more influential in fields other than his own.

Achievement in Context

The study of political theology is a narrow field, even among medieval historians.[3] Rather than starting a discussion about this subject, and how nations used political theology to construct themselves, in some ways the broad sweep of *The King's Two Bodies* brought the discussion to an end. It is the last major work on the subject in relation to medieval Western Europe.* When writing the book, Kantorowicz was an influential academic at the Institute of Advanced Studies in Princeton. This in itself meant the issue attracted the attention of other scholars in the field of history.

What was perhaps less predictable was that the book would be reprinted seven times, becoming important in many fields other than medieval history. Ironically, this was mainly down to parts of the book that were less warmly received when it was first published. Early readers of *The King's Two Bodies* enjoyed its wealth of learning and comprehensive referencing, but were less impressed by its methodology—specifically, the way it moved so freely between periods and drew on different media to comment on politics. In the decades that followed however, and particularly in other fields, it is *precisely* this depth of evidence, along with Kantorowicz's interest in the ways in which meaning is made, that has turned the the book into something more than a historical survey. Indeed, these things have ensured its lasting influence.

Limitations

Kantorowicz's ideas are exclusive and specific; it is his methodology that makes *The King's Two Bodies* universal. His ability to master a range of sources is a model for any historian. His key method is to identify the same terms when they are being used in different contexts, and to explore how their meanings either change or stay the same. Kantorowicz is interested in how an idea that appears to have a specific and limited application (an idea about the status of an abbot, for example) can be moved into another context for another application

47

(in this case, to justify the execution of a king). It is in areas like this that *The King's Two Bodies* becomes most universal, inviting readers to apply its ideas to different fields.

The book is still a work of its time, though, written in the 1950s by a historian whose formative years were the 1920s. The main cultural, rather than academic, criticism of Kantorowicz has been his rather unclear position in relation to Nazism.*[4] Despite his Polish Jewish background, Kantorowicz's early political sympathies were closer to Hitler's* than people might expect. It is possible to interpret *The King's Two Bodies* as identifying with the superiority of Western European culture and history given its almost total lack of interest in any country beyond the bounds of that geographical region. He does not begin to consider whether Europe may have been influenced by Middle Eastern or Indian ideas conveyed by Alexander the Great.* Nor does he consider how the king's two bodies* might be represented in eastern Europe, the Far East, or the global South. He does, however, speak consistently of "finding the source," of identifying the ultimate origin of this idea of royal or religious figures having two bodies.

Most modern historians would not consider it possible to identify the actual source of an idea; the consensus is that religion and power emerged out of long and complex processes connected with earlier civilizations elsewhere in the world. Perhapos because he was a product of the academic world of the early twentieth century, Kantorowicz never really considers this.

It could also be argued that Kantorowicz is really only interested in men; he does not discuss any female writers or artists in the work at all. And while it was in keeping with the cultural trends of Kantorowicz's own time, it is completely at odds with modern scholarship. The only woman who interests him is the English monarch Elizabeth I,* but she is discussed almost entirely as a monarch rather than as a woman. Only briefly, when discussing the iconography of the phoenix used by her court, does Kantorowicz mention Elizabeth's femininity.

NOTES

1 See, for instance, Ernst Kantorowicz, *The King's Two Bodies* (Princeton, NJ: Princeton University Press, 1997), xx.

2 See Bernhard Jussen's comments on the text's use as a sourcebook in Bernhard Jussen, "*The King's Two Bodies* Today," *Representations* 106, no. 1 (2009): 102–17, 104.

3 See, however, Hent de Vries and Lawrence E. Sullivan, eds, *Political Theologies* (New York: Fordham University Press, 2006).

4 Norman Cantor, "The Nazi Twins: Percy Ernst Schramm and Ernst Hartwig Kantorowicz," in *Inventing the Middle Ages: the Lives, Works, and Ideas of the Great Medievalists of the Twentieth Century*, ed. Norman Cantor (New York: Harper Collins, 1991), 79–117.

MODULE 8
PLACE IN THE AUTHOR'S WORK

KEY POINTS

- *The King's Two Bodies* is the culmination of Kantorowicz's work, bringing together theoretical ideas and vast learning from a lifetime of studying the medieval* period and its concerns.

- The book is recognizably part of Kantorowicz's body of work, focusing on the connections between economics and politics in history and the interactions between medieval law, theology, and kingship.

- Although his earlier biography of Frederick II* and some of his essays on legal history are still read today, *The King's Two Bodies* is by far Kantorowicz's most famous work.

Positioning

Although a volume of selected essays was published in 1965, two years after his death, *The King's Two Bodies* (1957) was Ernst Kantorowicz's last major completed work.[1] The subject of his first book, a 1927 biography of the medieval* German king Frederick II,* makes a significant appearance in *The King's Two Bodies*. For Kantorowicz, Frederick remained the supreme example of a monarch who was militarily successful, culturally sensitive, and intellectually productive.

Between these two books, much of Kantorowicz's work focused on the language of medieval kingship ceremonies, and particularly on how theological language and practices were incorporated into these ceremonies. This is most obvious in his book *Laudes Regiae: A Study in Liturgical Acclamations and Medieval Ruler Worship*.[2] As the subtitle suggests, this book examines how the Church and its ceremonies made medieval rulers semi-divine.* Kantorowicz builds on these ideas in *The King's Two Bodies*.

> ❝ It would go much too far, however, to assume that the author felt tempted to investigate the emergence of some of the idols of modern political religions merely on account of the horrifying experience of our own time in which whole nations, the largest and the smallest, fell prey to the weirdest dogmas and in which political theologisms became genuine obsessions defying in many cases the rudiments of human and political reason. ❞
>
> Ernst Kantorowicz, *The King's Two Bodies: A Study in Medieval Political Theology*

Although *The King's Two Bodies* stands apart from Kantorowicz's other works in its ambition and scope, his academic interests and his methods of investigation remained broadly consistent from first to last. This text, then, is best understood as a final summation of all his work, both absorbing and overwhelming.

Integration

Kantorowicz's first published work, his 1927 biography of Frederick II, reads completely differently from *The King's Two Bodies*. While the latter is characterized by a wealth of learning, often demonstrated in a "volcano" of footnotes,[3] the early work presents actual conclusions rather than simply research. It reads like a poetic, semi-mystical piece of adulation rather than a historical analysis. Intensely criticized for taking this approach, Kantorowicz published a companion volume in 1931 showing all the sources of the biography. It proved that Kantorowicz's research had been every bit as comprehensive as in his later work.[4]

The change in his approach writing the *The King's Two Bodies* may represent either a mellowing of his views in maturity or a continued reaction to the scorn heaped on his first book. And while its observations and conclusions can be disputed, Kantorowicz's sources are very much on display and his range of knowledge is clear.

While his method may have developed over the years, Kantorowicz's earlier publications are consistent in their subject matter. Even his university thesis of 1921 focused on the interactions between economics and politics in history. The interactions between medieval law, theology, and kingship, meanwhile, were always his key concerns. Kantorowicz developed a more specific interest in art and performance as building blocks of medieval power during the course of his career. This is perhaps most notably evident in *Laudes Regiae*.[5] Yet while he established the link between the arts and politics before *The King's Two Bodies*, his final work can be seen as encompassing, and in some ways overruling, all his previous publications.

Significance

The King's Two Bodies, the only one of his books still in print, is by some distance Kantorowicz's most important work—partly because it has been influential across such a range of disciplines. Art history has been strongly shaped by the links Kantorowicz suggests between artistic symbolism and political ideas, while the study of early modern* literature has been profoundly influenced by his reading of Shakespeare.* But perhaps his most significant impact has come from his interest in how meaning is created through language and image and how those meanings can be used to create and support power. These ideas have been very influential in philosophy and cultural studies. The fact that they continue to be so would appear to be primarily because of their influence on the renowned French philosopher Michel Foucault.*

When *The King's Two Bodies* was first published in 1957, Kantorowicz was secure and well known in his field. Yet without this book he would probably only be remembered as one of a number of scholarly mid-twentieth-century legal and constitutional historians. Because of it he inspired a range of disciplines, bringing the idea of the king's two bodies, an idea that fascinated him, to the forefront of people's minds in historical, artistic, and literary discussions of the medieval and early modern periods.

NOTES

1   Ernst Kantorowicz, *Selected Studies* (New York: J. J. Augustin, 1965).

2   Ernst Kantorowicz, *Laudes Regiae: A Study in Liturgical Acclamations and Medieval Ruler Worship, With a Study of the Music of the Laudes and Musical Transcriptions* (Berkeley, CA: University of California Press, 1946).

3   Stephen Greenblatt, "Introduction: Fifty Years of *The King's Two Bodies*," *Representations* 106, no. 1 (2009): 63–6, 64.

4   Ernst Kantorowicz, *Frederick the Second 1194–1250,* trans. E. O. Lorimer (New York: Frederick Ungar, 1957).

5   Kantorowicz, *Laudes Regiae*.

SECTION 3
IMPACT

MODULE 9
THE FIRST RESPONSES

KEY POINTS

- *The King's Two Bodies* was criticized for lacking a chronological approach, making it difficult to follow.

- Historians found the text and its footnotes to be a valuable work of reference. Philosophers and literary critics were interested in certain specific ideas.

- The most important scholar drawn to the book's ideas was the French philosopher Michel Foucault.*

Criticism

After the 1957 publication of *The King's Two Bodies: A Study in Medieval Political Theology*, critics and academics quickly recognized the significance and breadth of Ernst Kantorowicz's work. Its author was already a respected figure, so this distillation of his life's work and thinking was warmly welcomed.

The book's first audience, historians working in similar fields, was impressed by Kantorowicz's overwhelming knowledge and expertise; its intentionally comprehensive referencing and its lengthy footnotes, meanwhile, were recognized as a valuable source for both academics and students.

But academic historians of 1957 were not ready for the book's innovative structure, and it's non-chronological approach was challenging to most readers. The study of history was, in the main, the study of what had happened and how it had happened. Kantorowicz's primary interest, however—identifying how language and symbol construct ideas and meaning—required a different approach.

> ❝ This is a rich and muddled book. It would take a sabbatical term of hard labor to work through the more recent secondary sources quoted in the footnotes. Every medievalist will find something new there to interest him. It confuses because the author, as well as using esoteric diction, follows neither a chronological nor a systematic order. ❞
>
> Beryl Smalley, "Review of *The King's Two Bodies*"

Critics recognized the value of the sources, but did not always find it easy to identify exactly what the book as a whole was about. A review that found it "a rich and muddled" work which "confuses because the author … follows neither a chronological nor a systematic order" expressed a view that was by no means uncommon.[1]

The first critics of the text were all working in broadly the same fields as Kantorowicz—they were historians of the medieval* Church and state, some with more specialized positions within that broad spectrum. Kantorowicz himself was considered a senior figure in their field, and their criticisms were based on reactions to his unusual academic methodology. All agreed with Kantorowicz's view, given in his own preface, that *The King's Two Bodies* is an immensely valuable reference work. Historical scholars have generally agreed that the work that formed the foundations of *The King's Two Bodies* was inspiring in two ways— as a source for further study and as a model to be followed.[2]

Responses

The King's Two Bodies was the final academic achievement of Kantorowicz's life. He died in 1963 at the age of 68, six years after the book was published. He did not respond comprehensively to his critics and it is not certain whether or not he wanted to.

Kantorowicz did, however, continue to teach and work at Princeton. He delivered his last seminar, exploring the Italian poet Dante's* views on power in his work *De Monarchia*, in 1962.[3] Fittingly, the same subject occupies the final chapter of *The King's Two Bodies*—so it seems to be the case that Kantorowicz was still working on the same ideas, and using the same methods right up to the end of his career. One of the people who attended that last seminar recalls how Kantorowicz "sent us again and again" to the book and, in particular, to the "footnotes, which were the repository of his learning."[4]

The King's Two Bodies remains, then, Kantorowicz's final and comprehensive statement on his method and opinions.

Conflict and Consensus

There is no indication that Kantorowicz altered his ideas as a result of criticism of his work, and historians have generally agreed about its value. Over the 20 years or so that followed its publication, however, new academic fields developed and scholars working in these fields found themselves taken with Kantorowicz's interests beyond medieval history and statehood.

Ultimately, the readers who found most value in the book were not historians looking for a better understanding of medieval Europe. Philosophers and social thinkers found that it started them thinking about the ways in which culture, context, and language interact.[5] Art historians, particularly those interested in the medieval and early modern periods, found Kantorowicz's examination of the social and political functions of the visual arts appealing.[6] Literary critics, meanwhile, discovered a context-based approach to identifying key moments in literary works.[7] It is arguably in this final area that the book has had the most influence, making a great contribution to the birth of a school of literary theory specifically interested in these questions about the interaction of politics and literature—the New Historicist* school.

But *The King's Two Bodies'* most important reader was probably the French philosopher Michel Foucault, who was particularly interested in Kantorowicz's exploration of the king's physical body and the distinctions he draws between different types and values of bodies. As a result of Foucault's interest, cultural analysts, philosophers, and semioticians* —those who study how signs and symbols create meanings—were influenced by Kantorowicz's account of how symbols had been used for political ends.[8] Literary scholars read the chapter on Shakespeare;* art historians read the chapter on Christ-centered kingship; philosophers and jurists read "On Continuity and Corporations."

The way the book has been used tallies with what the earliest readers had argued: that there is much of value, but that its greatest strength is neither its organization nor its cohesion.

Almost 60 years after its publication, there is little agreement about *The King's Two Bodies* except that it is a rich source of inspiration and interest. There has, however, been a complete reversal of opinion from those first historians who found the content inspiring but the methodology clumsy. Nowadays the greatest value placed on the book is in its methods rather than its source material.

NOTES

1   Beryl Smalley, "Review of *The King's Two Bodies* by Ernst Kantorowicz," *Past & Present* 20 (1961): 30.

2   See Smalley, "Review;" compare Bernhard Jussen's discussion of the work's reception and use in Bernhard Jussen, "*The King's Two Bodies* Today," *Representations* 106, no. 1 (2009): 102–17 (especially 103–5), and William Chester Jordan, preface to Ernst Kantorowicz, *The King's Two Bodies* (Princeton, NJ: Princeton University Press, 1997).

3   For a discussion of Kantorowicz and Dante, see Kay E. Schiller, "Dante and Kantorowicz: Medieval History as Art and Autobiography," *Annali Italianistica* 8 (1990): 396–411.

4   The student is now Professor Michael Mahoney. See Jordan, preface to
    Kantorowicz, *The King's Two Bodies*, xiv.

5   For an overview, see Victoria Khan's "Political Theology and Fiction in *The
    King's Two Bodies*," *Representations* 106, no. 1 (2009): 77–101.

6   See Johannes Fried, "Ernst H. Kantorowicz and Postwar Historiography:
    German and European Perspectives," in *Ernst Kantorowicz: Erträge der
    Doppeltagung Princeton/ Frankfurt*, ed. Robert L. Benson and Johannes
    Fried (Stuttgart: Steiner, 1997), 180–201.

7   See, for instance, David Norbrook, "The Emperor's New Body? *Richard
    II*, Ernst Kantorowicz, and the Politics of Shakespeare Criticism," *Textual
    Practice* 10 (1996): 329–57, and, more generally, Stephen Greenblatt,
    "Introduction: Fifty Years of *The King's Two Bodies*," *Representations* 106,
    no. 1 (2009): 63–6.

8   See Jussen, "*The King's Two Bodies* Today," 104.

MODULE 10
THE EVOLVING DEBATE

KEY POINTS

- *The King's Two Bodies* influenced the increasing interest in academic methodologies and the need for theoretical frameworks to be established at the outset of a piece of work.

- With its focus on the interaction of different cultural media, the book can also be seen as having influenced the development of cultural studies.

- *The King's Two Bodies* can be seen as a founding text of New Historicism*—a school of literary theory that analyzes texts with specific reference to the contexts in which they were written.

Uses and Problems

Ernst Kantorowicz's *The King's Two Bodies: A Study in Medieval Political Theology* has had surprisingly little influence on the study of history. Since the 1950s, the academic study of history has generally involved increasingly focused and detailed examinations of specific periods and of ideas within their particular contexts. Perhaps this can be interpreted as a response to the Victorian* or early twentieth-century historical "grand survey," which, like *The King's Two Bodies*, covered a lengthy period of time.

People in different historical periods have different understandings of time, and there have been studies of the way these understandings change. But no historian since Kantorowicz would claim to have identified a single historical moment that saw "a change of man's sense of the nature of Time."[1] So no school in the field of history has formed around the ideas or the text.

❝ The book enjoyed success in academic fields beyond classical medieval history, particularly in experimental fields ... It seeded fruitful discussions among media archaeologists; sociologists; and scholars of modern literature, philosophy, political science, and cultural studies—the vast majority of whom were not medievalists. In short, what endures in today's debates is mainly an inspiration seeded by Kantorowicz's central image of the doubled body. **❞**

Bernhard Jussen, "*The King's Two Bodies* Today"

In the period since its publication in 1957, however, there have been a number of changes in the way historians work—and this text has arguably played a part in initiating and cultivating them. For instance, historians today are much more aware of the methodologies they choose and the impact those methodologies have on the work they produce. It is usual for historians to set out their theoretical interests in detail (that is, to describe their idea of how history works and should be analyzed) before or alongside the historical analysis itself. Kantorowicz is clearly moving in this direction in *The King's Two Bodies*. And while the work cannot be said to have been the single most important factor in this development, it has certainly played a role.

Writing the book, Kantorowicz's aim was also to develop an understanding of the interplay between different elements of culture. He focuses particularly on the way law, literature, and art actually construct meaning—and the ways those meanings can be controlled and manipulated for wider purposes. This is a way of studying semantics* (that is, the production of meaning). Since the publication of *The King's Two Bodies*, semantics has become a field in its own right and has played a major part in the evolution of the study of history. It has been especially significant in the growth of cultural studies,* the interdisciplinary field that examines how culture in all its forms can create and transform everyday life. This was not a specific subject at all in 1957, and *The King's Two Bodies* can claim to have been a powerful influence on this new academic field.

Certainly, the image of the king's two bodies* and the duality (that is, the "double nature") that it suggests in human nature has become a key area of discussion in cultural studies. It has led to wider debates about performance and reality that have affected subjects such as archaeology and costume studies, as well as law, history, literature, and art. It is not an overstatement to suggest that *The King's Two Bodies* has been a pivotal text for art history and literary studies. Much of this change came about as a result of the book's influence on one of the most significant philosophical thinkers of the twentieth century, Michel Foucault.* But it is also important to note that Kantorowicz sees works of literature and art as political (or at least potentially political) acts. In this sense, he was a strong influence on the New Historicist* movement, a school of literary theory that looks to describe how and why texts were produced and how their meaning has changed over time.

Schools of Thought

Kantorowicz's ideas have been the starting point for some of the most important modern fields of thinking.

Historians have largely rejected the idea of works looking at human nature across huge periods of time. But philosophers in the mid- to late twentieth century, most notably Michel Foucault, have used medieval* history to do precisely that. *The King's Two Bodies* has inspired the growth of cultural studies. Any modern work that looks at civilization through a combination of law, culture, personalities, and events is to some extent following on from Kantorowicz's principles.

This methodology, combined with Kantorowicz's sharp focus on the body and his ability to pick out interesting and symbolic events, has inspired a certain way of writing about humanity. However, it cannot be considered as a co-ordinated "school of thought."

The King's Two Bodies has also been a founding text in the area of New Historicism, specifically due to Kantorowicz's brief reading of the English playwright William Shakespeare's *Richard II** and his use of works of art. This field of academia focuses on understanding texts and artworks through the contexts of their production and how they were received at the time. In this it echoes Kantorowicz, who would try to understand how the same ideas could be adapted or presented in a legal document, a funeral ceremony, and a work of art. *The King's Two Bodies* was published about 20 years before New Historicism really took root. In that sense, it is more of a foundation than a direct inspiration—but it can certainly be seen as a central part of that school of thought.

In Current Scholarship
Scholars in a number of fields use Kantorowicz as a starting point for their own investigations. Given the wide scope of *The King's Two Bodies*, it is understandable that these people should come from a similarly wide range of fields including history, literary studies, contemporary politics, philosophy, and art history.[2] But these studies generally take Kantorowicz's principles and suggestions as starting points rather than directly engaging with the book itself.

There are, however, an increasing number of fields where ideas and methodology are used in ways that are similar to those of Kantorowicz himself. They too mostly explore nationhood and its creation and representation in cultural forms. The big difference is that they generally do so beyond medieval* Europe. Recent papers, for instance, consider "cosmic politics"*—the use of religious ideas for political purposes—in Buddhist* Siberia, and nationalism and masculinity in modern Turkey.[3] Kantorowicz's book is potentially relevant to discussions about national identity—particularly in the debate about the relative significance of ethnic, cultural, and religious markers.

Scholars examining the changing conceptual approaches to the bodies of royals have also brought Kantorowicz into play. In her edited collection *The Body of the Queen: Gender and Rule in the Courtly World, 1500–2000*, the German historian Regina Schulte* uses Kantorowicz as a point of departure to explore the roles of gender and the body of female monarchs up to the present day.[4] She argues that the natural body and the political body are intertwined in even more complex ways in iconography depicting queens than they are with kings.

NOTES

1   Ernst Kantorowicz, *The King's Two Bodies* (Princeton, NJ: Princeton University Press, 1997), 283.

2   Katherine Biddick, *Tears of Reign: Big Sovereigns Do Cry* (New York: Punctum Books, 2014); David Ciepley, "Beyond Public and Private: Toward a Political Theory of the Corporation," *American Political Science Review* 107, no. 1 (2013): 139–58; Kevin Bruyneel, "The King's Body: The Martin Luther King Jr. Memorial and the Politics of Collective Memory," *History and Memory* 26, no. 1 (2014): 75–108; Klaus Krüger, "Andrea Mantegna: Painting's Mediality," *Art History* 37, no. 2 (2014): 222–53.

3   Anya Bernstein, "More Alive Than All The Living: Sovereign Bodies and Cosmic Politics in Buddhist Siberia," *Cultural Anthropology* 27, no. 2 (2012): 261–85; Salih Can Açiksöz, "Sacrificial Limbs of Sovereignty: Disabled Veterans, Masculinity, and Nationalist Politics in Turkey," *Medical Anthropology Quarterly* 26, no. 1 (2012): 4–25.

4   See Regina Schulte, ed., *The Body of the Queen: Gender and Rule in the Courtly World, 1500–2000* (Oxford: Berghahn Books, 2006).

MODULE 11
IMPACT AND INFLUENCE TODAY

KEY POINTS

- *The King's Two Bodies* has been so widely used in its own field that it has become an authority—a point of reference—rather than an inspiration.

- Today, people look to apply the book's ideas in other areas, confirming conclusions about political and historical contexts by referencing a comparable breadth of cultural knowledge.

- There has been criticism that Kantorowicz is a Nazi* apologist—but this is generally seen as unfair.

Position

To an extent, Ernst Kantorowicz's *The King's Two Bodies: A Study in Medieval Political Theology* has been read, analyzed and used so comprehensively since its publication in 1957 that its lessons have now been thoroughly learned and applied. As a result, its immediate usefulness has declined and its historical, literary, and artistic analyses have been superseded by work that followed on from it. It remains informative, interesting, and foundational, but it is not directly inspirational.

Students of later thinkers such as the French philosopher Michel Foucault* and the Italian philosopher Umberto Eco* will find the patterns of their thinking and the events that concern them were anticipated by *The King's Two Bodies*. In early modern* literary criticism, the book was an inspiration to New Historicists* such as Stephen Greenblatt.* His thinking is instrumental to the current study of Renaissance* texts and New Historicism has been a powerful influence in literary and cultural studies.

> 66 The central image of the doubled body was doubtless successful, but the book's central concern about the political language predating and preparing 'the early modern commonwealths' was not. The vast majority of authors referring in one way or the other to *The King's Two Bodies* have used the book more as a source of inspiration than as a reference for a convincing narrative about constitutional history or an exemplary method for the study of political theory. 99
>
> Bernhard Jussen, "*The King's Two Bodies* Today"

Today the text is generally seen as the starting point in important fields of thinking. It is an essential reference point for any work on Shakespeare's* kings, on power in the medieval world, or on the formation of states in either the modern or medieval world. But *The King's Two Bodies* is also a classic work of scholarship in its own right.

It is fair to say, though, that it is very long, somewhat outdated and very specific in its immediate interests. As a result, it has become more of an authority than an inspiration—a book often owned, but less often read or cited. *The King's Two Bodies* established Ernst Kantorowicz as a significant figure, but he is no longer actively part of contemporary debate.

Interaction

The King's Two Bodies is still relevant in the continuing discussion of the role of the state and the nature of progress.

To a degree—and mostly outside the academic sphere—it confronts nationalist* ideologies by implying the artificiality (that is, the fictional notion) of any state. Kantorowicz does not see nations as inevitable or "true" groupings, but simply as constructed ideas. Nor does he see human history as a progressive development towards increasing civilization, but as a restless application of the same tools to the same ends of power and control.

His analysis focuses on the way symbols—linguistic, physical, performative, or visual—construct meaning. The implication is that there is no fundamental truth in what he explores. Meaning changes according to how useful it is to different people. The impact this had on the major thinkers of the 1960s and 1970s resulted in Kantorowicz's transformative ideas being mostly absorbed into academic debates rather than standing as a challenge to them. Indeed, "what endures in today's debates is mainly an inspiration seeded by Kantorowicz's central image of the doubled body,"[1] rather than a living debate about the value of his method or conclusions.

However, the challenge posed by *The King's Two Bodies* to the boundaries between academic subjects and traditional approaches to exploring history remains. Contemporary academic thinking is still mostly dominated by a straightforward exploration of key thinkers, works, and periods. The way Kantorowicz selects thinkers, writers and events from across time to identify patterns in language use—largely without an interest in their status in their own time—is not well thought of today. Kantorowicz would, perhaps, recognize today's wider intellectual debates more easily than he would those about historical study. Certainly, the intention of his text is to encourage wide engagement with, and application of, the different ideas he presents.

The Continuing Debate

While it is often cited, *The King's Two Bodies* is not a significant part of current debates. This is because its ideas have been so well absorbed into the academic fields of art history, history, cultural studies, and literary analysis.

Kantorowicz is an established figure, but also an old one, and his status has resulted in the person being challenged more than the writing. In particular, some people have criticized Kantorowicz's early right-wing inclinations, his opposition or otherwise to Nazi* policies, and his apparent total lack of interest in Eastern European and Jewish* history, politics, and culture. In fact, Kantorowicz is described as one of two "Nazi twins" in an influential essay, which is nowadays almost as well known as *The King's Two Bodies*.[2]

This essay was written by the historian Norman Cantor* who argues that, had Kantorowicz not been Jewish, he would himself have been a Nazi as his ideology and interests were closely allied with those of the Nazi party.

However, there is little justification for this view in Kantorowicz's life and work. He shared a sense of nationalism, a desire for strong leadership, and right-wing ideas with many intellectuals (from Germany and elsewhere) in the 1930s, and his biography of the German monarch Frederick II* was admired by Nazi leaders. However, there is no evidence that he agreed with Nazi ideas about race supremacy and, in fact, his own mother was murdered in the Holocaust.* Serious discussions of Kantorowicz's thinking and his engagement with Nazi policies are both more subtle in their understanding of the context in which he analyzes power and more certain of his opposition to Hitler's policies.[3]

From a more technical perspective, academics in different fields take issue with the way in which Kantorowicz uses sources and approaches without completely setting them in their contexts. *The King's Two Bodies* refers to art, literature, law, and events from a range of places and times as part of an overall argument about authority. It is perhaps inevitable that in doing so Kantorowicz does not always go into detail about the sources he cites. One of the most influential parts of the book is the second chapter, which uses Shakespeare's* *Richard II** to discuss ideas about the monarchy of Shakespeare's time, the Elizabethan* period.[4] While Kantorowicz's approach—of picking words and phrases from texts as evidence to support an argument—

has been widely adopted, it has also been criticized by people like the American literary critic Stephen Greenblatt.* Challengers to *The King's Two Bodies* want more detail and more contextualization of sources than that provided by the book.

NOTES

1   Bernard Jussen, "*The King's Two Bodies Today,*" Representations 106, no. 1 (2009), 105. The image of the doubled body is not, of course, originally Kantorowicz's: he takes it from Elizabethan law. Nor was he the first to write about it: the historian F. W. Maitland did so, in a work that Kantorowicz cites in his preface.

2   Norman Cantor, "The Nazi Twins: Percy Ernst Schramm and Ernst Hartwig Kantorowicz," in *Inventing the Middle Ages: the Lives, Works, and Ideas of the Great Medievalists of the Twentieth Century*, ed. Norman Cantor (New York: Harper Collins,1991), 79–117. In Jussen, "*The King's Two Bodies* Today," 103, Bernhard Jussen suggests that this piece is better known than Kantorowicz's own work.

3   Martin A. Ruehl. "'Imperium transcendat hominem': Reich and Rulership in Ernst Kantorowicz's *Kaiser Friedrich der Zweite,*" in *A Poet's Reich: Politics and Culture in the George Circle*, ed. Melissa S. Lane and Martin A. Ruehl (Woodbridge: Camden House, 2011), 223–5.

4   See, for instance, Richard Halpern, "The King's Two Buckets: Kantorowicz, *Richard II*, and Fiscal *Trauerspiel*," *Representations* 106, no. 1 (2009): 67–76; Lorna Hutson, "Imagining Justice: Kantorowicz and Shakespeare," *Representations* 106, no. 1 (2009): 118–42.

MODULE 12
WHERE NEXT?

KEY POINTS

- *The King's Two Bodies* has recently become influential in understanding how new states emerge. The application of its ideas about symbols and the creation of power is still relevant in, for instance, the political context of developing nations and in the ideological framework of the "War on Terror."*

- Specific chapters such as the discussion of Shakespeare* are still relevant to discussions of early modern* literature.

- Kantorowicz's work is still important because he identified the key questions: "What is power?" and "How is power used?"

Potential

The attention that Ernst Kantorowicz gave to the image of the king in *The King's Two Bodies* continues to inspire historians and academics in disciplines other than history.[1] He is still influential in early modern* literary criticism, where his analysis of Shakespeare's play *Richard II** is imitated, extended, challenged, and applied to a wider range of texts.[2] But *The King's Two Bodies* has been read, analyzed, and applied so comprehensively since its publication that its lessons have been well learned. As a result, its immediate usefulness has declined.

Today, readers are increasingly interested in asking what Kantorowicz's thinking and processes were. They are perhaps more interested in how he went about his writing rather than what he says in it.

Still, some of Kantorowicz's ideas have, as yet, barely influenced modern thinking. Core ideas of statehood and the manipulation of

> **"** [The] continuity of the people and the state derived from many sources, and in general it may be said that theory followed existing practice. Without depending on any broader philosophical outlooks the administrative technique of the state developed its own patterns of continuity. **"**
>
> Ernst Kantorowicz, *The King's Two Bodies: A Study in Medieval Political Theology*

theological ideas around the person of the ruler could still be explored a good deal further.[3] *The King's Two Bodies* has much to offer, for instance, in the controversial debate about the role of religion in politics, particularly in the Arab world.[4] Similarly, it could contribute to a contemporary exploration of the Anglo-Saxon monarchy* and its construction of the English nation through genealogies (that is, lines of descent traced from ancestors) and laws. Although Kantorowicz refers briefly to this topic,[5] he leaves room for further analysis and his text has the potential to again become important in this area.

In the wider world, there is perhaps even more potential. The text argues that the medieval* period laid the foundations of the modern period and that the two are closely connected. But the non-academic world continues to view this period as the Dark Ages.* If anything, the medieval period is today represented as being further away and more "other" than it was when Kantorowicz was working: barbaric and primitive or mystical and magical—but in no sense part of the modern world. Kantorowicz believes a proper understanding of the context in which an idea has currency is essential if that idea is not to appear "meaningless" or, worse, "ludicrous."[6] Yet this is precisely how contemporary culture regularly presents events and ideas from the Middle Ages.

Future Directions

Kantorowicz has few disciples but many admirers, mainly because of the age of his work. His early followers have now gone in directions of their own and there is little need to work closely with *The King's Two Bodies* when it has been absorbed and supplanted. His work is not as outdated as many of the historical "grand surveys" produced by his contemporaries, but nor is it as cutting-edge or radical as later studies. Kantorowicz's sheer breadth of knowledge is impressive and his skill at handling sources remarkable. His arguments, meanwhile, are always interesting at the very least, but this is a question of reference and discussion rather then re-engagement.

Kantorowicz's analysis continues to be applied to different Shakespearean texts and other literary works in research led by the English literary scholar David Norbrook* and the American literary critic Stephen Greenblatt.* These applications often follow Kantorowicz's interest in the play *Richard II** or approach other plays from a similar viewpoint, although such studies largely ignore his wider argument.[7]

A range of thinkers still engage with Kantorowicz's ideas about monarchs and their bodies, or political theology* and statehood, or the political status of corporations.[8] Kantorowicz is cited in those discussions and his are ideas acknowledged as foundational. But *The King's Two Bodies* no longer takes center stage academically; the German historian Bernard Jussen* speaks of the text's "grandchildren,"[9] and it is through these works, by followers of Kantorowicz, where the text is found to be useful today.

Summary

The King's Two Bodies deserves special attention for several reasons. It comes out of interesting, specific historical circumstances; it represents a lifetime of study; it is readable and enjoyable; it has influenced a range of fields and thinkers; and it is radical in considering the nature and the construction of power. At the very least, the text offers the reader fascinating anecdotes discussed by an excited author. At best, it demonstrates an originality of methodology and a control of varied source material that could be a model for any student.

The text may be most important now for the people and movements it influenced rather than its actual content. Nevertheless, a work on medieval constitutional* history that so deeply influenced philosophy, literary study, cultural studies, and art history deserves to be acknowledged.

As a work of historical research it is still relevant. It analyzes the many factors that shape our understanding of what a state is and is ambitious in tracing an idea across many centuries and places. *The King's Two Bodies* brings an immense range of material to the attention of academics; it organizes that material and offers it as a source for further exploration. In the process, it makes a case for the ongoing value of ideas and the understanding of the way power is extended across places and times.

The King's Two Bodies, and the ideas it contains, are defined by the way Kantorowicz approaches his work. It is partly due to his efforts that historians are obliged today to consider culture as broadly as they do.

His influence can also be seen in the increased focus on how ideas and people are represented, or how meaning is produced (that is, in semantics)* rather than in any fundamental nature they might possess. Kantorowicz is not particularly interested, for example, in what makes a good king; his focus is on the many ways an individual could be represented to portray himself as a "good king" according to contemporary ideas about what being a good king meant.

Although this principle was taken further in later decades, it is a particularly interesting feature of *The King's Two Bodies*—a text where a vast range of historical knowledge allows that notion to be applied and extended so far across time and place.

NOTES

1   See Bernhard Jussen, "*The King's Two Bodies* Today," *Representations* 106, no. 1 (2009): 104 for a list of some of the titles he describes as the text's "first grandchildren."

2   See, for instance, James Phillips, "The Practicalities of the Absolute: Justice and Kingship in Shakespeare's *Richard II*," *English Literary History* 79, no. 1 (2012): 161–77; Lorna Hutson, "Imagining Justice: Kantorowicz and Shakespeare," *Representations* 106, no. 1 (2009): 118–42.

3   See Jussen, "*The King's Two Bodies* Today," where this argument is strongly made.

4   See, for example, David Nirenberg, "'Judaism' as Political Concept: Toward a Critique of Political Theology," *Representations* 128, no. 1 (2014): 1–29.

5   Ernst Kantorowicz, *The King's Two Bodies* (Princeton, NJ: Princeton University Press, 1997), 312–13.

6   Kantorowicz, *The King's Two Bodies*, 3, 5.

7   See, for instance, Phillips, "The Practicalities of the Absolute."

8   Katherine Biddick, *Tears of Reign: Big Sovereigns Do Cry* (New York: Punctum Books, 2014); Nirenberg, "Judaism," 1–29; David Ciepley, "Beyond Public and Private: Toward a Political Theory of the Corporation," *American Political Science Review* 107, no. 1 (2013): 139–58.

9   Jussen, "*The King's Two Bodies* Today."

GLOSSARY

GLOSSARY OF TERMS

Ancient Egypt: a civilization of northern Africa, roughly in the same place as modern Egypt, which lasted as an independent empire from around 3100 to 30 B.C.E. when it was conquered and became a part of the Roman Empire.

Buddhist: a way of living based mostly on the teachings of Gautama Buddha, who lived in eastern Asia around the fifth century B.C.E. Buddhism focuses on eliminating desires as the source of suffering and fear, and is often connected with meditation, calm, and peacefulness. Buddhists seek to discover and accept their place in the cosmos rather than pursuing immediate, human, desires.

Classical period: the name given to the empires of Greece and Rome that preceded the medieval period in Western Europe. Like most historical labels, its precise boundaries are quite vague, but it is usually dated from around the eighth century B.C.E. to around the sixth century C.E.

Cold War: usually dated from 1947 until 1991, this was a long period of tension and enmity between Eastern and Western powers and, in particular, between the Soviet Union and the United States.

Communism: an ideal that all citizens in a state should be equal and that the ideal should be imposed by removing markers of difference—such as money, class, and religion—from society. Versions of communism have been used to govern countries across the world, most notably the Soviet Union and China.

Constantinople: originally called Byzantium, now Istanbul. From 330 until 1453 (apart from a brief break in the period 1204 to 1261), it was a major city of the Roman Empire and capital of the empire in eastern Europe.

Constitutional historians: a constitution describes the basis of a nation state and can set the limits of the state's power over its individual citizens. Constitutional historians study the development of state powers and the laws describing them.

Constitutional semantics: the study of how ideas about the structure of authority in nations are created and shifted through the use of words and images.

Cosmic politics: a term meaning roughly the same as "political theology": the use of religious ideas for political purposes. The term has been used specifically to describe this process in a Buddhist culture, where Christian theological ideas do not apply and mystical thinking is linked more to the idea of the cosmos.

Cosmos: the idea of the universe as an ordered whole. In a religious context, it is often connected with Buddhist thinking.

Cultural studies: a field of academic study developed in England in the second half of the twentieth century. It seeks to understand how contemporary cultures work and the different forces that affect people's everyday lives within different cultural settings.

Dark Ages: often used to describe the period between the end of the Western Roman Empire around 400 C.E. and the growth of nation states in Western Europe★ around 800 C.E. The period is "dark" because there is comparatively little written or archaeological evidence to understand the period better.

Divine: that which is connected to a supernatural power, usually a god. Things that are called divine usually share the attributes of a god, such as being outside the sphere of human understanding, being permanent, and being in some sense "truer" or more real than mere human experience.

Duality: being made up of two parts. It is often used to describe two opposing forces, such as light and dark, or the body and the mind. The two parts of a duality are not necessarily opposed.

Early medieval period: a European period usually dated from approximately 400 C.E. until approximately 1000 C.E.

Early modern period: a broad term for the time after the end of the medieval period and before the start of the industrialized modern period. Precise date boundaries vary depending on how it is defined, but it is usually seen as lasting roughly from the discovery of America in 1492 to the French Revolution in 1789.

Elizabethan: relating to the reign of the English monarch Elizabeth I (1533–1603). Elizabeth was queen of England from 1558 until 1603, and is widely seen as having reigned during an English "golden age"—a period where England became a dominant power, with significant military, economic and cultural advances.

Enlightenment: a lengthy period in philosophical history, usually dated from 1637 (when Descartes published his *Discourse on Method*) until about 1789 (when the French Revolution began). Its influence on science and other academic pursuits lasted much longer.

Holocaust: A systematic program run by the Nazis that killed ethnic and social minorities in Europe, primarily Jewish people. More than six million Jews, around four million Slavs and thousands of Romani people, homosexuals and those with disabilities were all murdered, many at purpose-built extermination camps.

Holy Roman Empire: a group of kingdoms first united as an empire under Charlemagne, who was crowned as an emperor by the Pope in 800 C.E. This is why his empire was called "Holy" and "Roman." Its boundaries changed regularly over time but were similar to those of modern Germany.

Islamism: the principle that the Islamic faith should guide nations as well as individuals: that laws, government, society, and culture should be based on Islam.

King's two bodies: the concept of a monarch being a physical person and an abstract idea at one and the same time. A king is both a human being and a representation of a country.

McCarthyism: a period of political repression in the United States lasting roughly 1950–57 and named after Senator Joseph McCarthy. Also called the Red Scare, it tried to root out communists, especially those who might be spying for the Soviet Union. The term is often used today to mean a process of making allegations against individuals for political repression and control.

Medieval period: also known as the Middle Ages, the medieval period is generally considered to last from the fifth to the fifteenth century. It is so called as it is the middle of the three common divisions in European history: the Classical period, the Middle Ages, and the modern period.

Metaphysical: relating to the study of abstract ideas such as "truth" and "power" and the exploration of the most fundamental aspects of human existence, such as "time" and "being."

Nationalist: the identification of the needs of an individual or group of ethnically similar individuals with a particular nation state, often resulting in absolute devotion to the needs of that state and the exclusion of other ethnic groups from it.

Nazi: led by Adolf Hitler, the Nazis took power in Germany in 1933 and ruled until 1945. They are generally regarded as having caused the outbreak of World War II. During the course of that war, they committed war crimes including the Holocaust.

New Historicism: an academic movement based on the study of literature which seeks to describe how and why texts were produced when they were, and how and why their meaning has shifted over time according to changing historical contexts.

Parliament: the supreme legal authority in the United Kingdom, which can create or end any law. It is made up of the House of Commons, the House of Lords, and the sovereign.

Political theology: describes how states and rulers use mythical and religious language and structures to extend power over their subjects.

Red Scare: the name given to the extreme fear and persecution of left-wing thinkers in the United States due to their connection with the communist Soviet Union, America's enemy during the Cold War. It is usually dated from approximately 1947 until 1957 and is also called McCarthyism, after Senator Joseph McCarthy.

Reformation: a sixteenth-century movement that led to a schism in European Christianity. It began as an attempt to reform the Church and eventually led to a split between the Protestant and Catholic Christian traditions.

Renaissance: the Renaissance was a period in European history strongly influenced by Classical ideas about art and literature. It occupied the same time frame as the early modern period; indeed, the terms are often used interchangeably.

Semantics: the study of meaning and how it is made. It focuses on language and other symbols and how they work together to create different meanings.

Semioticians: those who study semantics, the use of signs and symbols and the ways in which they can create meaning. Michel Foucault is probably the best-known semiotician.

Soviet Union, or USSR: a kind of "super state" that existed from 1922 to 1991, centered primarily on Russia and its neighbors in Eastern Europe and the northern half of Asia. It was the communist pole of the Cold War, with the United States as its main "rival".

Theology: the study of religious beliefs and practices.

Victorian: relating to the reign of Queen Victoria (1819–1901), queen of the United Kingdom between 1837 and 1901. Her long reign saw a huge expansion of the British Empire and significant industrial and scientific developments.

War on Terror: the term most commonly applied to the various military campaigns and foreign policy actions that have taken place since the coordinated terrorist attacks on the United States of September 11, 2001, masterminded by Osama Bin Laden, the leader of the militant Islamist organization al-Qaeda.

Weimar Republic: the governing system of Germany from 1919. It is named after Weimar, where the constitutional assembly met that drew up the republican system. It is usually seen as ending in 1933 when Adolf Hitler seized power, but officially the same constitution lasted until 1945.

Western Europe: broadly, the countries in the western half of the European continent including the UK, France, Germany, and Italy among others. It roughly corresponds to the western half of the Classical Roman Empire.

World War I: a war lasting from 1914 to 1918 and principally a conflict between the Austro-Hungarian and German empires on one side and the British, French and Russian empires on the other. The nations initially involved all had complex systems of alliances and, as a result, many states around the world entered into the conflict, resulting in around 20 million deaths.

World War II: usually dated from 1939 to 1945, although conflict between China and Japan started before that. Like World War I, what started as a European conflict between Germany and her neighbors resulted in the eruption of tensions around the world and about 50 million deaths before it was brought to an end.

PEOPLE MENTIONED IN THE TEXT

Alexander the Great (356–323 B.C.E.) was king of Macedon in northern Greece from 336 until 323 B.C.E. He led armies east across Asia and into northern Africa. Undefeated in battle, he created a huge empire. He died at the age of 32 and his empire was swiftly broken apart by civil war.

Friedrich Baethgen (1892–1972) was a German historian. A specialist on the medieval papacy, he is best known for being the president of the German historical series *Monumenta Germaniae Historica* from 1948 to 1959.

Charles Beard (1874–1948) was an influential American historian and teacher. He was a leading figure in the progressive school of historiography, focusing on economic class conflict. He most famously wrote *An Economic Interpretation of the Constitution of the United States*.

Reinhard Bendix (1916–91) was a German sociologist who emigrated to the United States in 1938. He is sometimes credited with bringing the idea of comparative historical studies to the United States, particularly supporting the analysis of American history in relation to European nations.

Marc Bloch (1886–1944) was a French medieval historian. He is best known today for *The Historian's Craft*, published in 1988. Kantorowicz would have known his *French Rural History* and *The Royal Touch*, which explores the mythic powers attributed to medieval kings.

Ernst Cassirer (1874–1945) was a German philosopher who wrote about the power of symbols and myths, most famously in *Philosophy of*

Symbolic Forms and *The Myth of the State.* His work was a significant influence on Kantorowicz.

Charlemagne (742–814 c.e.) became Holy Roman Emperor in 800, ruling over the lands which are now mostly in Germany, Italy and France. His capital was in Aachen in north-west Germany.

Charles I (1600–49) was king of England from 1625 to 1649. The English Civil War was fought in part as a reaction against his autocratic rule. He was executed in 1649.

Durante degli Alighieri, usually called Dante (1265–1321) was an Italian poet whose most famous work is the *Divine Comedy* (*La Divina Commedia* in Italian). He was interested in the twin spheres of politics and religion, which he discusses in his poetry and in his work *De Monarchia* ("On Monarchy").

Umberto Eco (b. 1932) is an Italian philosopher and writer. Best known as a novelist, his texts often explore the varied uses made of sign and symbol in the medieval world. His novel *Baudolino* explores myth as part of the construction of authority in a way that Kantorowicz may have recognized.

Edward VI (1537–53) became king of England in 1547 at the age of nine. As Henry VIII's only surviving son he was heir to the throne of England ahead of his older sisters Mary and Elizabeth. He was succeeded by Mary I.

Elizabeth I (1533–1603) was queen of England between 1558 and 1603. She is widely seen as having reigned during a "golden age"—a period in which England became a dominant power, with significant military, economic and cultural advances.

Carl Erdmann (1898–1945) was a German historian who worked on medieval political history and the development of ideas. He died relatively young in World War II★ and so has not had the impact of his contemporaries. An English translation of his *The Origin of the Idea of Crusade* by Marshall W. Baldwin and Walter Goffart was published in 1977.

Michel Foucault (1926–84) was a French philosopher who notably explored the nature and workings of power, among many other subjects. His most significant works are probably *Discipline and Punish: The Birth of the Prison* and *A History of Sexuality*. In *Discipline and Punish*, he claims to be working "in homage to Kantorowicz."

Frederick II (1194–1250) was a medieval king of Germany and Holy Roman Emperor. His realm covered modern Sicily, Italy and Germany and even, briefly, Jerusalem. Although his dynasty did not last long beyond his death, he is a dominant figure in German history because of his personal energy, power, and interest in culture.

Stefan George (1868–1933) was a poet who used mystical ideas and images. His ideas about heroism, power, and German national identity were influential on many different groups, including the Nazis and those who resisted them. His best-known work today is probably *Das Neue Reich* ("The New Empire").

Joseph Goebbels (1897–1945) was one of Hitler's closest associates. Extremely anti-Semitic, he is noted for being responsible for the Nazis' propaganda program.

Johann Wolfgang von Goethe (1749–1832) was most famous as a German poet, playwright, and dramatist; he also wrote philosophy, science, and literary criticism. His most famous work today is the play

Faust, which retells an old story of a man who sells his soul to the Devil.

Stephen Greenblatt (b. 1943) is an American literary critic, largely regarded as one of the founders of the New Historicist movement. His best-known works include *Renaissance Self-Fashioning: From More to Shakespeare* and *Practicing New Historicism*.

Friedrich Gundolf (1880–1931) was a German Jewish literary scholar and poet, and, like Kantorowicz, a member of the circle around the poet Stefan George. Anticipating the ideas of the New Historicists, he was interested in literature in its historical context, most famously seeing writers such as Goethe as embedded in their own time.

Karl Hampe (1869–1936) researched the early medieval German Empire. His most significant book was published in English as *Germany under the Salic and Hohenstaufen Emperors*.

Adolf Hitler (1889–1945) was leader of Germany as chancellor and then dictator from 1933 to 1945. Under his leadership, German foreign policy became extremely aggressive, leading to World War II, and his domestic policy, including the implementation of the Holocaust, was repressive and cruel.

Bernard Jussen (b. 1959) is a German historian focused on the medieval period. His most significant work translated into English is probably *Spiritual Kinship as Social Practice*, a work dealing with godparenthood and adoption in the early Middle Ages.

Frederick William Maitland (1850–1906) was a legal historian, generally regarded as the founder of that discipline. His most significant work is *The Constitutional History of England*, published in 1909.

Joseph McCarthy (1908–57) was an American politician and senator, who started and sustained the Red Scare★ with claims that communists were infiltrating American society.

David Norbrook (b. 1950) is an English literary scholar who explores early modern literature and its intersections with history and politics. His most significant work to date is *Poetry and Politics in the English Renaissance*.

Max Radin (1880–1950) was born into a Jewish family in Poland but went to the United States in 1884. He studied Classical Greek and Roman law. He was interested in how the language of law influenced literature, and inspired Kantorowicz's interest in the legal status of corporations.

Carl Schmitt (1888–1985) was a political theorist and jurist. He was highly controversial because of his support for Nazi policies and anti-communist dictatorship. His most influential work is probably *The Concept of the Political*. His thinking is often referred to when discussing whether extraordinary measures can be taken to address extraordinary threats as in, for instance, the so-called War on Terror.

Percy Ernst Schramm (1894–1970) was a German historian of medieval politics and ritual. He was an officer in World War II and worked with Hitler.★ As a result, some of his work is less highly regarded than it might otherwise have been. His *History of the English Coronation* was translated into English in 1937.

Regina Schulte (b. 1949) is a German historian focused on social history and the role of women. Her best-known work in English is probably *The Village in Court: Arson, Infanticide, and Poaching in the Court Records of Upper Bavaria 1848–1910*.

William Shakespeare (1564–1616) worked mostly as a playwright in London. His texts dominate English literature. Thirty-nine plays are currently attributed to him, including comedies, tragedies, histories, and romances. Kantorowicz and his followers have been mostly interested in his histories, which portray different English kings.

WORKS CITED

WORKS CITED

Açiksöz, Salih Can. "Sacrificial Limbs of Sovereignty: Disabled Veterans, Masculinity, and Nationalist Politics in Turkey." *Medical Anthropology Quarterly* 26, no. 1 (2012): 4–25.

Bates, David. "Political Theology and the Nazi State: Carl Schmitt's Concept of the Institution." *Modern Intellectual History* 3 (2006): 415–42.

Beard, Charles. *An Economic Interpretation of the Constitution of the United States*. New York: MacMillan, 1913.

Bernstein, Anya. "More Alive Than All The Living: Sovereign Bodies and Cosmic Politics in Buddhist Siberia." *Cultural Anthropology* 27, no. 2 (2012): 261–85.

Biddick, Katherine. *Tears of Reign: Big Sovereigns Do Cry*. New York: Punctum Books, 2014.

Bloch, Marc. *French Rural History.* Translated by Peter Putnam. Manchester: Manchester University Press, 1954.

The Royal Touch. Translated by J. E. Anderson. London: Routledge and Kegan Paul, 1973.

Bruyneel, Kevin. "The King's Body: The Martin Luther King Jr. Memorial and the Politics of Collective Memory." *History and Memory* 26, no. 1 (2014): 75–108.

Cantor, Norman. "The Nazi Twins: Percy Ernst Schramm and Ernst Hartwig Kantorowicz." In *Inventing the Middle Ages: The Lives, Works, and Ideas of the Great Medievalists of the Twentieth Century*, edited by Norman Cantor. New York: Harper Collins, 1991.

Cassirer, Ernst. *The Myth of the State*. New Haven, CT: Yale University Press, 1946.

The Philosophy of Symbolic Forms. Vol. 1, *Language*. Translated by Ralph Manheim. New Haven, CT: Yale University Press, 1955.

The Philosophy of Symbolic Forms. Vol. 2, *Mythical Thought*. Translated by Ralph Manheim. New Haven, CT: Yale University Press, 1965.

The Philosophy of Symbolic Forms. Vol. 3, *The Phenomenology of Knowledge*. Translated by Ralph Manheim. New Haven, CT: Yale University Press, 1965.

The Philosophy of the Enlightenment. Translated by Fritz C. A. Koelln and James P. Pettegrove. Princeton, NJ: Princeton University Press, 1964.

Ciepley, David. "Beyond Public and Private: Toward a Political Theory of the Corporation." *The American Political Science Review* 107, no. 1 (2013): 139–58.

de Vries, Hent, and Lawrence E. Sullivan, eds. *Political Theologies*. New York: Fordham University Press, 2006.

Eco, Umberto. *Baudolino*. Orlando, FL: Harcourt, 2000.

Erdmann, Carl. *The Origin of the Idea of Crusade*. Translated by Marshall W. Baldwin and Walter Goffart. Princeton, NJ: Princeton University Press, 1977.

Fried, Johannes. "Ernst H. Kantorowicz and Postwar Historiography: German and European Perspectives". In *Ernst Kantorowicz: Erträge der Doppeltagung Princeton/Frankfurt*, edited by Robert L. Benson and Johannes Fried, 180–201. Stuttgart: F. Steiner, 1997.

Foucault, Michel. *Discipline and Punish: The Birth of the Prison,* 2nd edn. Translated by Alan Sheridan. New York: Vintage, 1975.

A History of Sexuality. 3 vols. Translated by Robert Hurley. London: Allen Lane, 1976–84.

Gallagher, Catherine, and Stephen Greenblatt. *Practicing New Historicism*. Chicago: University of Chicago Press, 2000.

George, Stefan. *Das Neue Reich*. Berlin: Georg Bondi, 1928.

Greenblatt, Stephen. *Renaissance Self-Fashioning: From More to Shakespeare,* 2nd edn. Chicago: University of Chicago Press, 2005.

"Introduction: Fifty Years of *The King's Two Bodies*." *Representations* 106, no. 1 (2009): 63–6.

Halpern, Richard. "The King's Two Buckets: Kantorowicz, *Richard II*, and Fiscal *Trauerspiel*." *Representations* 106, no. 1 (2009): 67–76.

Hampe, Karl. *Germany under the Salic and Hohenstaufen Emperors.* Lanham, MD: Rowman and Littlefield, 1973.

Hutson, Lorna. "Imagining Justice: Kantorowicz and Shakespeare." *Representations* 106, no. 1 (2009): 118–42.

Jussen, Bernhard. "*The King's Two Bodies* Today." *Representations* 106, no. 1 (2009): 102–17.

Kahn, Victoria. "Political Theology and Fiction in *The King's Two Bodies*." *Representations* 106, no. 1 (2009): 77–101.

Kantorowicz, Ernst H. *Kaiser Friedrich der Zweite*. Berlin: Georg Bondi, 1927.

Laudes Regiae: A Study in Liturgical Acclamations and Medieval Ruler Worship With a Study of the Music of the Laudes and Musical Transcriptions. Berkeley, CA: University of California Press, 1946.

Frederick the Second 1194–1250. Translated by E. O. Lorimer. New York: Frederick Ungar, 1957.

Selected Studies. New York: J. J. Augustin, 1965.

The King's Two Bodies: A Study in Mediaeval Political Theology. Princeton, NJ: Princeton University Press, 1997.

Krüger, Klaus. "Andrea Mantegna: Painting's Mediality." *Art History* 37, no. 2 (2014): 222–53.

Maitland, F. W. *The Constitutional History of England.* Cambridge: Cambridge University Press, 1909.

Nirenberg, David. "'Judaism' as Political Concept: Toward a Critique of Political Theology." *Representations* 128, no. 1 (2014): 1–29.

Norbrook, David. "The Emperor's New Body? *Richard II*, Ernst Kantorowicz, and the Politics of Shakespeare Criticism." *Textual Practice* 10 (1996): 329–57.

Poetry and Politics in the English Renaissance. Oxford: Oxford University Press, 2002.

Phillips, James. "The Practicalities of the Absolute: Justice and Kingship in Shakespeare's *Richard II*." *English Literary History* 79, no. 1 (2012): 161–77.

Ruehl, Martin. "In This Time Without Emperors: The Politics of Ernst Kantorowicz's *Friedrich der Zweite* Reconsidered." *Journal of the Warburg and Courtauld Institutes* 63 (2000): 187–242.

Schiller, Kay E. "Dante and Kantorowicz: Medieval History as Art and Autobiography." *Annali Italianistica* 8 (1990): 396–411.

Schmitt, Carl. *Politische Theologie. Vier Kapitel zur Lehre von der Souveränität.* Berlin: Duncker & Humblot, 1922.

Political Theology: Four Chapters on the Concept of Sovereignty. Translated by George Schwab. Cambridge, MA: MIT Press, 1985.

The Concept of the Political. Translated by George Schwab. Chicago: University of Chicago Press, 2007.

Schramm, Percy Ernst. *History of the English Coronation.* Translated by Leopold Legg. Oxford: Clarendon Press, 1937.

Schulte, Regina, ed. *The Body of the Queen: Gender and Rule in the Courtly World, 1500–2000.* Oxford: Berghahn Books, 2006.

Smalley, Beryl. "Review of *The King's Two Bodies* by Ernst Kantorowicz." *Past and Present* 20 (1961): 30–5.

Stroup, John. "Political Theology and Secularization Theory in Germany, 1918–1939: Emmanuel Hirsch as a Phenomenon of His Time." *Harvard Theological Review* 80, no. 3 (1987): 321–68.

Tal, Uriel. "On Structures of Political Theology and Myth Prior to the Holocaust." In *The Holocaust as Historical Experience*, edited by Yehuda Bauer and Nathan Rotenstreich, 43–74. New York: Holmes and Meier, 1981.

THE MACAT LIBRARY
BY DISCIPLINE

AFRICANA STUDIES

Chinua Achebe's *An Image of Africa: Racism in Conrad's Heart of Darkness*
W. E. B. Du Bois's *The Souls of Black Folk*
Zora Neale Huston's *Characteristics of Negro Expression*
Martin Luther King Jr's *Why We Can't Wait*
Toni Morrison's *Playing in the Dark: Whiteness in the American Literary Imagination*

ANTHROPOLOGY

Arjun Appadurai's *Modernity at Large: Cultural Dimensions of Globalisation*
Philippe Ariès's *Centuries of Childhood*
Franz Boas's *Race, Language and Culture*
Kim Chan & Renée Mauborgne's *Blue Ocean Strategy*
Jared Diamond's *Guns, Germs & Steel: the Fate of Human Societies*
Jared Diamond's *Collapse: How Societies Choose to Fail or Survive*
E. E. Evans-Pritchard's *Witchcraft, Oracles and Magic Among the Azande*
James Ferguson's *The Anti-Politics Machine*
Clifford Geertz's *The Interpretation of Cultures*
David Graeber's *Debt: the First 5000 Years*
Karen Ho's *Liquidated: An Ethnography of Wall Street*
Geert Hofstede's *Culture's Consequences: Comparing Values, Behaviors, Institutes and Organizations across Nations*
Claude Lévi-Strauss's *Structural Anthropology*
Jay Macleod's *Ain't No Makin' It: Aspirations and Attainment in a Low-Income Neighborhood*
Saba Mahmood's *The Politics of Piety: The Islamic Revival and the Feminist Subject*
Marcel Mauss's *The Gift*

BUSINESS

Jean Lave & Etienne Wenger's *Situated Learning*
Theodore Levitt's *Marketing Myopia*
Burton G. Malkiel's *A Random Walk Down Wall Street*
Douglas McGregor's *The Human Side of Enterprise*
Michael Porter's *Competitive Strategy: Creating and Sustaining Superior Performance*
John Kotter's *Leading Change*
C. K. Prahalad & Gary Hamel's *The Core Competence of the Corporation*

CRIMINOLOGY

Michelle Alexander's *The New Jim Crow: Mass Incarceration in the Age of Colorblindness*
Michael R. Gottfredson & Travis Hirschi's *A General Theory of Crime*
Richard Herrnstein & Charles A. Murray's *The Bell Curve: Intelligence and Class Structure in American Life*
Elizabeth Loftus's *Eyewitness Testimony*
Jay Macleod's *Ain't No Makin' It: Aspirations and Attainment in a Low-Income Neighborhood*
Philip Zimbardo's *The Lucifer Effect*

ECONOMICS

Janet Abu-Lughod's *Before European Hegemony*
Ha-Joon Chang's *Kicking Away the Ladder*
David Brion Davis's *The Problem of Slavery in the Age of Revolution*
Milton Friedman's *The Role of Monetary Policy*
Milton Friedman's *Capitalism and Freedom*
David Graeber's *Debt: the First 5000 Years*
Friedrich Hayek's *The Road to Serfdom*
Karen Ho's *Liquidated: An Ethnography of Wall Street*

The Macat Library By Discipline

John Maynard Keynes's *The General Theory of Employment, Interest and Money*
Charles P. Kindleberger's *Manias, Panics and Crashes*
Robert Lucas's *Why Doesn't Capital Flow from Rich to Poor Countries?*
Burton G. Malkiel's *A Random Walk Down Wall Street*
Thomas Robert Malthus's *An Essay on the Principle of Population*
Karl Marx's *Capital*
Thomas Piketty's *Capital in the Twenty-First Century*
Amartya Sen's *Development as Freedom*
Adam Smith's *The Wealth of Nations*
Nassim Nicholas Taleb's *The Black Swan: The Impact of the Highly Improbable*
Amos Tversky's & Daniel Kahneman's *Judgment under Uncertainty: Heuristics and Biases*
Mahbub Ul Haq's *Reflections on Human Development*
Max Weber's *The Protestant Ethic and the Spirit of Capitalism*

FEMINISM AND GENDER STUDIES

Judith Butler's *Gender Trouble*
Simone De Beauvoir's *The Second Sex*
Michel Foucault's *History of Sexuality*
Betty Friedan's *The Feminine Mystique*
Saba Mahmood's *The Politics of Piety: The Islamic Revival and the Feminist Subject*
Joan Wallach Scott's *Gender and the Politics of History*
Mary Wollstonecraft's *A Vindication of the Rights of Woman*
Virginia Woolf's *A Room of One's Own*

GEOGRAPHY

The Brundtland Report's *Our Common Future*
Rachel Carson's *Silent Spring*
Charles Darwin's *On the Origin of Species*
James Ferguson's *The Anti-Politics Machine*
Jane Jacobs's *The Death and Life of Great American Cities*
James Lovelock's *Gaia: A New Look at Life on Earth*
Amartya Sen's *Development as Freedom*
Mathis Wackernagel & William Rees's *Our Ecological Footprint*

HISTORY

Janet Abu-Lughod's *Before European Hegemony*
Benedict Anderson's *Imagined Communities*
Bernard Bailyn's *The Ideological Origins of the American Revolution*
Hanna Batatu's *The Old Social Classes And The Revolutionary Movements Of Iraq*
Christopher Browning's *Ordinary Men: Reserve Police Batallion 101 and the Final Solution in Poland*
Edmund Burke's *Reflections on the Revolution in France*
William Cronon's *Nature's Metropolis: Chicago And The Great West*
Alfred W. Crosby's *The Columbian Exchange*
Hamid Dabashi's *Iran: A People Interrupted*
David Brion Davis's *The Problem of Slavery in the Age of Revolution*
Nathalie Zemon Davis's *The Return of Martin Guerre*
Jared Diamond's *Guns, Germs & Steel: the Fate of Human Societies*
Frank Dikotter's *Mao's Great Famine*
John W Dower's *War Without Mercy: Race And Power In The Pacific War*
W. E. B. Du Bois's *The Souls of Black Folk*
Richard J. Evans's *In Defence of History*
Lucien Febvre's *The Problem of Unbelief in the 16th Century*
Sheila Fitzpatrick's *Everyday Stalinism*

Eric Foner's *Reconstruction: America's Unfinished Revolution, 1863-1877*
Michel Foucault's *Discipline and Punish*
Michel Foucault's *History of Sexuality*
Francis Fukuyama's *The End of History and the Last Man*
John Lewis Gaddis's *We Now Know: Rethinking Cold War History*
Ernest Gellner's *Nations and Nationalism*
Eugene Genovese's *Roll, Jordan, Roll: The World the Slaves Made*
Carlo Ginzburg's *The Night Battles*
Daniel Goldhagen's *Hitler's Willing Executioners*
Jack Goldstone's *Revolution and Rebellion in the Early Modern World*
Antonio Gramsci's *The Prison Notebooks*
Alexander Hamilton, John Jay & James Madison's *The Federalist Papers*
Christopher Hill's *The World Turned Upside Down*
Carole Hillenbrand's *The Crusades: Islamic Perspectives*
Thomas Hobbes's *Leviathan*
Eric Hobsbawm's *The Age Of Revolution*
John A. Hobson's *Imperialism: A Study*
Albert Hourani's *History of the Arab Peoples*
Samuel P. Huntington's *The Clash of Civilizations and the Remaking of World Order*
C. L. R. James's *The Black Jacobins*
Tony Judt's *Postwar: A History of Europe Since 1945*
Ernst Kantorowicz's *The King's Two Bodies: A Study in Medieval Political Theology*
Paul Kennedy's *The Rise and Fall of the Great Powers*
Ian Kershaw's *The "Hitler Myth": Image and Reality in the Third Reich*
John Maynard Keynes's *The General Theory of Employment, Interest and Money*
Charles P. Kindleberger's *Manias, Panics and Crashes*
Martin Luther King Jr's *Why We Can't Wait*
Henry Kissinger's *World Order: Reflections on the Character of Nations and the Course of History*
Thomas Kuhn's *The Structure of Scientific Revolutions*
Georges Lefebvre's *The Coming of the French Revolution*
John Locke's *Two Treatises of Government*
Niccolò Machiavelli's *The Prince*
Thomas Robert Malthus's *An Essay on the Principle of Population*
Mahmood Mamdani's *Citizen and Subject: Contemporary Africa And The Legacy Of Late Colonialism*
Karl Marx's *Capital*
Stanley Milgram's *Obedience to Authority*
John Stuart Mill's *On Liberty*
Thomas Paine's *Common Sense*
Thomas Paine's *Rights of Man*
Geoffrey Parker's *Global Crisis: War, Climate Change and Catastrophe in the Seventeenth Century*
Jonathan Riley-Smith's *The First Crusade and the Idea of Crusading*
Jean-Jacques Rousseau's *The Social Contract*
Joan Wallach Scott's *Gender and the Politics of History*
Theda Skocpol's *States and Social Revolutions*
Adam Smith's *The Wealth of Nations*
Timothy Snyder's *Bloodlands: Europe Between Hitler and Stalin*
Sun Tzu's *The Art of War*
Keith Thomas's *Religion and the Decline of Magic*
Thucydides's *The History of the Peloponnesian War*
Frederick Jackson Turner's *The Significance of the Frontier in American History*
Odd Arne Westad's *The Global Cold War: Third World Interventions And The Making Of Our Times*

LITERATURE

Chinua Achebe's *An Image of Africa: Racism in Conrad's Heart of Darkness*
Roland Barthes's *Mythologies*
Homi K. Bhabha's *The Location of Culture*
Judith Butler's *Gender Trouble*
Simone De Beauvoir's *The Second Sex*
Ferdinand De Saussure's *Course in General Linguistics*
T. S. Eliot's *The Sacred Wood: Essays on Poetry and Criticism*
Zora Neale Huston's *Characteristics of Negro Expression*
Toni Morrison's *Playing in the Dark: Whiteness in the American Literary Imagination*
Edward Said's *Orientalism*
Gayatri Chakravorty Spivak's *Can the Subaltern Speak?*
Mary Wollstonecraft's *A Vindication of the Rights of Women*
Virginia Woolf's *A Room of One's Own*

PHILOSOPHY

Elizabeth Anscombe's *Modern Moral Philosophy*
Hannah Arendt's *The Human Condition*
Aristotle's *Metaphysics*
Aristotle's *Nicomachean Ethics*
Edmund Gettier's *Is Justified True Belief Knowledge?*
Georg Wilhelm Friedrich Hegel's *Phenomenology of Spirit*
David Hume's *Dialogues Concerning Natural Religion*
David Hume's *The Enquiry for Human Understanding*
Immanuel Kant's *Religion within the Boundaries of Mere Reason*
Immanuel Kant's *Critique of Pure Reason*
Søren Kierkegaard's *The Sickness Unto Death*
Søren Kierkegaard's *Fear and Trembling*
C. S. Lewis's *The Abolition of Man*
Alasdair MacIntyre's *After Virtue*
Marcus Aurelius's *Meditations*
Friedrich Nietzsche's *On the Genealogy of Morality*
Friedrich Nietzsche's *Beyond Good and Evil*
Plato's *Republic*
Plato's *Symposium*
Jean-Jacques Rousseau's *The Social Contract*
Gilbert Ryle's *The Concept of Mind*
Baruch Spinoza's *Ethics*
Sun Tzu's *The Art of War*
Ludwig Wittgenstein's *Philosophical Investigations*

POLITICS

Benedict Anderson's *Imagined Communities*
Aristotle's *Politics*
Bernard Bailyn's *The Ideological Origins of the American Revolution*
Edmund Burke's *Reflections on the Revolution in France*
John C. Calhoun's *A Disquisition on Government*
Ha-Joon Chang's *Kicking Away the Ladder*
Hamid Dabashi's *Iran: A People Interrupted*
Hamid Dabashi's *Theology of Discontent: The Ideological Foundation of the Islamic Revolution in Iran*
Robert Dahl's *Democracy and its Critics*
Robert Dahl's *Who Governs?*
David Brion Davis's *The Problem of Slavery in the Age of Revolution*

Alexis De Tocqueville's *Democracy in America*
James Ferguson's *The Anti-Politics Machine*
Frank Dikotter's *Mao's Great Famine*
Sheila Fitzpatrick's *Everyday Stalinism*
Eric Foner's *Reconstruction: America's Unfinished Revolution, 1863-1877*
Milton Friedman's *Capitalism and Freedom*
Francis Fukuyama's *The End of History and the Last Man*
John Lewis Gaddis's *We Now Know: Rethinking Cold War History*
Ernest Gellner's *Nations and Nationalism*
David Graeber's *Debt: the First 5000 Years*
Antonio Gramsci's *The Prison Notebooks*
Alexander Hamilton, John Jay & James Madison's *The Federalist Papers*
Friedrich Hayek's *The Road to Serfdom*
Christopher Hill's *The World Turned Upside Down*
Thomas Hobbes's *Leviathan*
John A. Hobson's *Imperialism: A Study*
Samuel P. Huntington's *The Clash of Civilizations and the Remaking of World Order*
Tony Judt's *Postwar: A History of Europe Since 1945*
David C. Kang's *China Rising: Peace, Power and Order in East Asia*
Paul Kennedy's *The Rise and Fall of Great Powers*
Robert Keohane's *After Hegemony*
Martin Luther King Jr.'s *Why We Can't Wait*
Henry Kissinger's *World Order: Reflections on the Character of Nations and the Course of History*
John Locke's *Two Treatises of Government*
Niccolò Machiavelli's *The Prince*
Thomas Robert Malthus's *An Essay on the Principle of Population*
Mahmood Mamdani's *Citizen and Subject: Contemporary Africa And The Legacy Of Late Colonialism*
Karl Marx's *Capital*
John Stuart Mill's *On Liberty*
John Stuart Mill's *Utilitarianism*
Hans Morgenthau's *Politics Among Nations*
Thomas Paine's *Common Sense*
Thomas Paine's *Rights of Man*
Thomas Piketty's *Capital in the Twenty-First Century*
Robert D. Putman's *Bowling Alone*
John Rawls's *Theory of Justice*
Jean-Jacques Rousseau's *The Social Contract*
Theda Skocpol's *States and Social Revolutions*
Adam Smith's *The Wealth of Nations*
Sun Tzu's *The Art of War*
Henry David Thoreau's *Civil Disobedience*
Thucydides's *The History of the Peloponnesian War*
Kenneth Waltz's *Theory of International Politics*
Max Weber's *Politics as a Vocation*
Odd Arne Westad's *The Global Cold War: Third World Interventions And The Making Of Our Times*

POSTCOLONIAL STUDIES

Roland Barthes's *Mythologies*
Frantz Fanon's *Black Skin, White Masks*
Homi K. Bhabha's *The Location of Culture*
Gustavo Gutiérrez's *A Theology of Liberation*
Edward Said's *Orientalism*
Gayatri Chakravorty Spivak's *Can the Subaltern Speak?*

PSYCHOLOGY

Gordon Allport's *The Nature of Prejudice*
Alan Baddeley & Graham Hitch's *Aggression: A Social Learning Analysis*
Albert Bandura's *Aggression: A Social Learning Analysis*
Leon Festinger's *A Theory of Cognitive Dissonance*
Sigmund Freud's *The Interpretation of Dreams*
Betty Friedan's *The Feminine Mystique*
Michael R. Gottfredson & Travis Hirschi's *A General Theory of Crime*
Eric Hoffer's *The True Believer: Thoughts on the Nature of Mass Movements*
William James's *Principles of Psychology*
Elizabeth Loftus's *Eyewitness Testimony*
A. H. Maslow's *A Theory of Human Motivation*
Stanley Milgram's *Obedience to Authority*
Steven Pinker's *The Better Angels of Our Nature*
Oliver Sacks's *The Man Who Mistook His Wife For a Hat*
Richard Thaler & Cass Sunstein's *Nudge: Improving Decisions About Health, Wealth and Happiness*
Amos Tversky's *Judgment under Uncertainty: Heuristics and Biases*
Philip Zimbardo's *The Lucifer Effect*

SCIENCE

Rachel Carson's *Silent Spring*
William Cronon's *Nature's Metropolis: Chicago And The Great West*
Alfred W. Crosby's *The Columbian Exchange*
Charles Darwin's *On the Origin of Species*
Richard Dawkin's *The Selfish Gene*
Thomas Kuhn's *The Structure of Scientific Revolutions*
Geoffrey Parker's *Global Crisis: War, Climate Change and Catastrophe in the Seventeenth Century*
Mathis Wackernagel & William Rees's *Our Ecological Footprint*

SOCIOLOGY

Michelle Alexander's *The New Jim Crow: Mass Incarceration in the Age of Colorblindness*
Gordon Allport's *The Nature of Prejudice*
Albert Bandura's *Aggression: A Social Learning Analysis*
Hanna Batatu's *The Old Social Classes And The Revolutionary Movements Of Iraq*
Ha-Joon Chang's *Kicking Away the Ladder*
W. E. B. Du Bois's *The Souls of Black Folk*
Émile Durkheim's *On Suicide*
Frantz Fanon's *Black Skin, White Masks*
Frantz Fanon's *The Wretched of the Earth*
Eric Foner's *Reconstruction: America's Unfinished Revolution, 1863-1877*
Eugene Genovese's *Roll, Jordan, Roll: The World the Slaves Made*
Jack Goldstone's *Revolution and Rebellion in the Early Modern World*
Antonio Gramsci's *The Prison Notebooks*
Richard Herrnstein & Charles A Murray's *The Bell Curve: Intelligence and Class Structure in American Life*
Eric Hoffer's *The True Believer: Thoughts on the Nature of Mass Movements*
Jane Jacobs's *The Death and Life of Great American Cities*
Robert Lucas's *Why Doesn't Capital Flow from Rich to Poor Countries?*
Jay Macleod's *Ain't No Makin' It: Aspirations and Attainment in a Low Income Neighborhood*
Elaine May's *Homeward Bound: American Families in the Cold War Era*
Douglas McGregor's *The Human Side of Enterprise*
C. Wright Mills's *The Sociological Imagination*

Thomas Piketty's *Capital in the Twenty-First Century*
Robert D. Putman's *Bowling Alone*
David Riesman's *The Lonely Crowd: A Study of the Changing American Character*
Edward Said's *Orientalism*
Joan Wallach Scott's *Gender and the Politics of History*
Theda Skocpol's *States and Social Revolutions*
Max Weber's *The Protestant Ethic and the Spirit of Capitalism*

THEOLOGY

Augustine's *Confessions*
Benedict's *Rule of St Benedict*
Gustavo Gutiérrez's *A Theology of Liberation*
Carole Hillenbrand's *The Crusades: Islamic Perspectives*
David Hume's *Dialogues Concerning Natural Religion*
Immanuel Kant's *Religion within the Boundaries of Mere Reason*
Ernst Kantorowicz's *The King's Two Bodies: A Study in Medieval Political Theology*
Søren Kierkegaard's *The Sickness Unto Death*
C. S. Lewis's *The Abolition of Man*
Saba Mahmood's *The Politics of Piety: The Islamic Revival and the Feminist Subject*
Baruch Spinoza's *Ethics*
Keith Thomas's *Religion and the Decline of Magic*

COMING SOON

Chris Argyris's *The Individual and the Organisation*
Seyla Benhabib's *The Rights of Others*
Walter Benjamin's *The Work Of Art in the Age of Mechanical Reproduction*
John Berger's *Ways of Seeing*
Pierre Bourdieu's *Outline of a Theory of Practice*
Mary Douglas's *Purity and Danger*
Roland Dworkin's *Taking Rights Seriously*
James G. March's *Exploration and Exploitation in Organisational Learning*
Ikujiro Nonaka's *A Dynamic Theory of Organizational Knowledge Creation*
Griselda Pollock's *Vision and Difference*
Amartya Sen's *Inequality Re-Examined*
Susan Sontag's *On Photography*
Yasser Tabbaa's *The Transformation of Islamic Art*
Ludwig von Mises's *Theory of Money and Credit*

Macat Disciplines

Access the greatest ideas and thinkers across entire disciplines, including

INEQUALITY

Ha-Joon Chang's, *Kicking Away the Ladder*

David Graeber's, *Debt: The First 5000 Years*

Robert E. Lucas's, *Why Doesn't Capital Flow from Rich To Poor Countries?*

Thomas Piketty's, *Capital in the Twenty-First Century*

Amartya Sen's, *Inequality Re-Examined*

Mahbub Ul Haq's, *Reflections on Human Development*

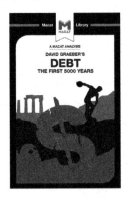

Macat Disciplines

Access the greatest ideas and thinkers across entire disciplines, including

CRIMINOLOGY

Michelle Alexander's
The New Jim Crow:
Mass Incarceration in the
Age of Colorblindness

Michael R. Gottfredson
& Travis Hirschi's
A General Theory of Crime

Elizabeth Loftus's
Eyewitness Testimony

Richard Herrnstein
& Charles A. Murray's
The Bell Curve: Intelligence and
Class Structure in American Life

Jay Macleod's
Ain't No Makin' It:
Aspirations and Attainment in a
Low-Income Neighborhood

Philip Zimbardo's
The Lucifer Effect

Macat analyses are available from all good bookshops and libraries.

Access hundreds of analyses through one, multimedia tool.
Join free for one month **library.macat.com**

Macat Pairs

Analyse historical and modern issues from opposite sides of an argument. Pairs include:

HOW TO RUN AN ECONOMY

John Maynard Keynes's
The General Theory OF Employment, Interest and Money

Classical economics suggests that market economies are self-correcting in times of recession or depression, and tend toward full employment and output. But English economist John Maynard Keynes disagrees.

In his ground-breaking 1936 study *The General Theory*, Keynes argues that traditional economics has misunderstood the causes of unemployment. Employment is not determined by the price of labor; it is directly linked to demand. Keynes believes market economies are by nature unstable, and so require government intervention. Spurred on by the social catastrophe of the Great Depression of the 1930s, he sets out to revolutionize the way the world thinks

Milton Friedman's
The Role of Monetary Policy

Friedman's 1968 paper changed the course of economic theory. In just 17 pages, he demolished existing theory and outlined an effective alternate monetary policy designed to secure 'high employment, stable prices and rapid growth.'

Friedman demonstrated that monetary policy plays a vital role in broader economic stability and argued that economists got their monetary policy wrong in the 1950s and 1960s by misunderstanding the relationship between inflation and unemployment. Previous generations of economists had believed that governments could permanently decrease unemployment by permitting inflation—and vice versa. Friedman's most original contribution was to show that this supposed trade-off is an illusion that only works in the short term.

Macat Disciplines

Access the greatest ideas and thinkers across entire disciplines, including

THE FUTURE OF DEMOCRACY

Robert A. Dahl's, *Democracy and Its Critics*
Robert A. Dahl's, *Who Governs?*
Alexis De Toqueville's, *Democracy in America*
Niccolò Machiavelli's, *The Prince*
John Stuart Mill's, *On Liberty*
Robert D. Putnam's, *Bowling Alone*
Jean-Jacques Rousseau's, *The Social Contract*
Henry David Thoreau's, *Civil Disobedience*

Macat Disciplines

Access the greatest ideas and thinkers across entire disciplines, including

TOTALITARIANISM

Sheila Fitzpatrick's, *Everyday Stalinism*
Ian Kershaw's, *The "Hitler Myth"*
Timothy Snyder's, *Bloodlands*

Macat Pairs

Analyse historical and modern issues from opposite sides of an argument. Pairs include:

RACE AND IDENTITY

Zora Neale Hurston's
Characteristics of Negro Expression

Using material collected on anthropological expeditions to the South, Zora Neale Hurston explains how expression in African American culture in the early twentieth century departs from the art of white America. At the time, African American art was often criticized for copying white culture. For Hurston, this criticism misunderstood how art works. European tradition views art as something fixed. But Hurston describes a creative process that is alive, ever-changing, and largely improvisational. She maintains that African American art works through a process called 'mimicry'—where an imitated object or verbal pattern, for example, is reshaped and altered until it becomes something new, novel—and worthy of attention.

Frantz Fanon's
Black Skin, White Masks

Black Skin, White Masks offers a radical analysis of the psychological effects of colonization on the colonized.

Fanon witnessed the effects of colonization first hand both in his birthplace, Martinique, and again later in life when he worked as a psychiatrist in another French colony, Algeria. His text is uncompromising in form and argument. He dissects the dehumanizing effects of colonialism, arguing that it destroys the native sense of identity, forcing people to adapt to an alien set of values—including a core belief that they are inferior. This results in deep psychological trauma.

Fanon's work played a pivotal role in the civil rights movements of the 1960s.

Macat analyses are available from all good bookshops and libraries.

Access hundreds of analyses through one, multimedia tool.
Join free for one month **library.macat.com**

Macat Pairs

Analyse historical and modern issues from opposite sides of an argument. Pairs include:

INTERNATIONAL RELATIONS IN THE 21ST CENTURY

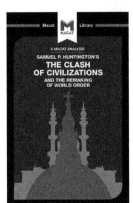

Samuel P. Huntington's
The Clash of Civilisations

In his highly influential 1996 book, Huntington offers a vision of a post-Cold War world in which conflict takes place not between competing ideologies but between cultures. The worst clash, he argues, will be between the Islamic world and the West: the West's arrogance and belief that its culture is a "gift" to the world will come into conflict with Islam's obstinacy and concern that its culture is under attack from a morally decadent "other."

Clash inspired much debate between different political schools of thought. But its greatest impact came in helping define American foreign policy in the wake of the 2001 terrorist attacks in New York and Washington.

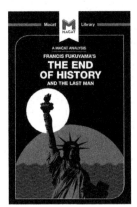

Francis Fukuyama's
The End of History and the Last Man

Published in 1992, *The End of History and the Last Man* argues that capitalist democracy is the final destination for all societies. Fukuyama believed democracy triumphed during the Cold War because it lacks the "fundamental contradictions" inherent in communism and satisfies our yearning for freedom and equality. Democracy therefore marks the endpoint in the evolution of ideology, and so the "end of history." There will still be "events," but no fundamental change in ideology.

Macat Disciplines

Access the greatest ideas and thinkers across entire disciplines, including

MAN AND THE ENVIRONMENT

The Brundtland Report's, *Our Common Future*
Rachel Carson's, *Silent Spring*
James Lovelock's, *Gaia: A New Look at Life on Earth*
Mathis Wackernagel & William Rees's, *Our Ecological Footprint*

Macat analyses are available from all good bookshops and libraries.

Access hundreds of analyses through one, multimedia tool.
Join free for one month **library.macat.com**

Macat Pairs

Analyse historical and modern issues from opposite sides of an argument. Pairs include:

ARE WE FUNDAMENTALLY GOOD - OR BAD?

Steven Pinker's
The Better Angels of Our Nature

Stephen Pinker's gloriously optimistic 2011 book argues that, despite humanity's biological tendency toward violence, we are, in fact, less violent today than ever before. To prove his case, Pinker lays out pages of detailed statistical evidence. For him, much of the credit for the decline goes to the eighteenth-century Enlightenment movement, whose ideas of liberty, tolerance, and respect for the value of human life filtered down through society and affected how people thought. That psychological change led to behavioral change—and overall we became more peaceful. Critics countered that humanity could never overcome the biological urge toward violence; others argued that Pinker's statistics were flawed.

Philip Zimbardo's
The Lucifer Effect

Some psychologists believe those who commit cruelty are innately evil. Zimbardo disagrees. In *The Lucifer Effect*, he argues that sometimes good people do evil things simply because of the situations they find themselves in, citing many historical examples to illustrate his point. Zimbardo details his 1971 Stanford prison experiment, where ordinary volunteers playing guards in a mock prison rapidly became abusive. But he also describes the tortures committed by US army personnel in Iraq's Abu Ghraib prison in 2003—and how he himself testified in defence of one of those guards. committed by US army personnel in Iraq's Abu Ghraib prison in 2003—and how he himself testified in defence of one of those guards.

Macat analyses are available from all good bookshops and libraries.

Access hundreds of analyses through one, multimedia tool.
Join free for one month **library.macat.com**

Macat Pairs

Analyse historical and modern issues from opposite sides of an argument. Pairs include:

HOW WE RELATE TO EACH OTHER AND SOCIETY

Jean-Jacques Rousseau's
The Social Contract

Rousseau's famous work sets out the radical concept of the 'social contract': a give-and-take relationship between individual freedom and social order.

If people are free to do as they like, governed only by their own sense of justice, they are also vulnerable to chaos and violence. To avoid this, Rousseau proposes, they should agree to give up some freedom to benefit from the protection of social and political organization. But this deal is only just if societies are led by the collective needs and desires of the people, and able to control the private interests of individuals. For Rousseau, the only legitimate form of government is rule by the people.

Robert D. Putnam's
Bowling Alone

In *Bowling Alone*, Robert Putnam argues that Americans have become disconnected from one another and from the institutions of their common life, and investigates the consequences of this change.

Looking at a range of indicators, from membership in formal organizations to the number of invitations being extended to informal dinner parties, Putnam demonstrates that Americans are interacting less and creating less "social capital" – with potentially disastrous implications for their society.

It would be difficult to overstate the impact of *Bowling Alone*, one of the most frequently cited social science publications of the last half-century.

Macat analyses are available from all good bookshops and libraries.

Access hundreds of analyses through one, multimedia tool.
Join free for one month **library.macat.com**

Printed in the United States
by Baker & Taylor Publisher Services